101 CUSTOMER SERVICE TRAINING

Quick and Easy Techniques That Get Great Results

THIRD EDITION

Renée Evenson

AMACOM

AMERICAN MANAGEMENT ASSOCIATION

New York • Atlanta • Brussels • Chicago • Mexico City • San Francisco
Shanghai • Tokyo • Toronto • Washington, D.C.

Bulk discounts available. For details visit:
www.amacombooks.org/go/specialsales
Or contact special sales:
Phone: 800-250-5308
E-mail: specialsls@amanet.org
View all the AMACOM titles at: www.amacombooks.org

American Management Association: www.amanet.org
This publication is designed to provide accurate and authoritative information in regard to the subject matter covered. It is sold with the understanding that the publisher is not engaged in rendering legal, accounting, or other professional service. If legal advice or other expert assistance is required, the services of a competent professional person should be sought.

Library of Congress Cataloging-in-Publication Data
Names: Evenson, Renee, 1951- author.
Title: Customer service training 101 : quick and easy techniques that get
    great results / Renee Evenson.
Description: Third edition. | Includes index.
Identifiers: LCCN 2017015093 (print) | LCCN 2017028110 (ebook) | ISBN
    9780814438923 (eBook) | ISBN 9780814438916 (pbk.)
Subjects: LCSH: Customer services. | Customer relations. |
    Employees--Training of.
Classification: LCC HF5415.5 (ebook) | LCC HF5415.5 .E89 2018 (print) | DDC
    658.3/1245--dc23
LC record available at https://lccn.loc.gov/2017015093

About AMA
American Management Association (www.amanet.org) is a world leader in talent development, advancing the skills of individuals to drive business success. Our mission is to support the goals of individuals and organizations through a complete range of products and services, including classroom and virtual seminars, webcasts, webinars, podcasts, conferences, corporate and government solutions, business books, and research. AMA's approach to improving performance combines experiential learning—learning through doing—with opportunities for ongoing professional growth at every step of one's career journey.

10 9 8 7 6 5 4 3 2 1

CONTENTS

PART I

PUTTING YOUR BEST FACE FORWARD

1 Your First Steps Can Make a Huge Stride: The Basics *19*

2 Tossing the Ball Back and Forth: Effective Communication *41*

PART II

PUTTING YOUR CUSTOMERS FIRST

PART III

PUTTING IT ALL TOGETHER

ACKNOWLEDGMENTS

My deep appreciation to . . .

My editor, **Tim Burgard**. Thank you for asking me to write this third edition. I value your insight and helpful suggestions as we worked together on this book.

My agent, **Michael Snell**. Thank you for representing my works and always watching out for my best interests. You have been my toughest critic and give me great advice that is always on target.

The team at **AMACOM Books**. I am so appreciative that you gave me the opportunity to write the first edition of *Customer Service Training 101*, published in 2005. Since the publication of that book, AMACOM has published all of my business books, and I am thankful to you for giving me that first opportunity that has blossomed into a long-term relationship.

My managing editor, **Anna Melhorn**, and the team at **Neuwirth & Associates**, for their expertise in copyediting and producing this edition.

My **clients and readers**. I would not be a writer without all of you. I listen closely to your feedback and always try to give you the best customer service.

My deepest appreciation is to **my family**. My husband, my daughters and their families, and my brother and his family are all inspirations to me. For each of you, I always strive to be my best and be an inspiration to you. Love to all of you.

Introduction

It was interesting rereading the introductions to the first two editions of this book. In 2005, when the first edition was published, the book focused on competition in the global economy at a time when consumers were becoming comfortable with conducting business via the Internet. The marketplace was expanding universally and consumers were discovering that they had unlimited choices. Providing exceptional service was even more important than it had been in the past, for the simple reason that customers who were not satisfied with the way they were treated could easily take their business elsewhere.

The introduction for the second edition, published in 2010, was written at a time when we were coming out of the worst recession in a generation. The stark reality was that millions of businesses had closed their doors. Consumer confidence was at an all-time low, which meant that providing exceptional customer service was now a necessity for keeping the business doors open. At the time the second edition was written, self-service options were becoming popular. A new chapter on providing service in self-serve situations was added, to teach how to provide a great customer experience when customers least expected it.

At that time, Facebook and Twitter were fledgling start-ups and played no role in business. Fast-forward to today, when social media is considered the customer service of the future. And the future is today. While Facebook and Twitter are still the most widely utilized networks, many others have flooded the Internet and will continue to do so. Businesses are realizing that these networks provide a valuable tool in customer service and support functions. Many consumers prefer the speed in communicating with a company via social media networks—as long as businesses are on board and up to speed with responding and providing expedient customer service. This precipitated the need for an updated version of the book.

Customer Service Training 101, 3rd edition, has been completely updated with an emphasis on the various ways customer service is provided in today's marketplace. While some customers still rely on in-person and phone interactions, we are definitely moving toward a future where we post our questions and complaints on social media networks and utilize live-chat options to communicate with companies. A new chapter, "Keeping Up with the Times: Online and Social Media Customer Service," emphasizes how best to respond to and interact with customers when writing is the means of communication. The focus of this chapter is on teaching the importance of good writing skills in social media, email, and chat interactions.

In addition, each chapter includes:

- The wrong way/right way to handle contacts

- Tips and topics for brainstorm discussions

- *Business NOT as Usual,* which provides ideas and tips for sustaining your business and growing your customer base

- A Practice Lesson

- *Doing It Right!,* which highlights a personal experience story

- *How Do I Measure Up?,* which asks thought-provoking questions to help you analyze your skill level

Every component of learning how to interact well with customers, no matter the means of communication, is included:

- Displaying courtesy and respect by making a great first impression, speaking, behaving, and writing appropriately, maintaining a positive attitude, and acting ethically

■ Communicating well by saying what you mean to say, projecting proper nonverbal signals, asking and answering questions correctly, and listening well

■ Building strong relationships by establishing rapport, interacting positively with customers, identifying needs, and finding the best solution

■ Handling customers well in face-to-face, telephone, Internet and social media, and self-service settings

■ Handling customer complaints to satisfaction

Customer service training benefits everyone involved, from your customers to your employees to your management team. Well-trained employees are your key to success. When your employees know how to find the best solution for each customer, you increase your chances of developing loyal customers. This book provides you with the tools to train your employees to find those best solutions. Whether you are reading this book for the first time or already own the first or second edition, this updated version is your one-stop shop to learn and teach how to give exceptional customer service.

We are living in an era in which technology is moving at such a rapid pace it can make our heads spin trying to keep up with the latest developments. AI (artificial intelligence) chatbots are beginning to play a role in handling rudimentary customer service needs. Even though chatbots may eventually handle many basic interactions, I believe consumers will always prefer the human "touch" when it comes to providing exceptional customer service. And that is the main reason that *Customer Service Training 101* will always benefit you and your employees, now and tomorrow.

Tips for the Trainer

**TRAINING SESSIONS SHOULD
BE A POSITIVE EXPERIENCE
FOR BOTH THE TRAINER AND THE TRAINEE**

Your most important role as a trainer is to ensure that the frontline employees you are training learn the fundamentals of providing exceptional customer service to every customer all the time. Investing the time to train your employees can be a fun and positive experience for both you and them. The key to holding successful training classes lies in preparation. Preparing before you begin will help you feel comfortable and confident and will take the guesswork out of your expectations. Preparation includes identifying your training needs, defining learning outcomes, planning your teaching lessons, establishing time frames for training sessions, preparing yourself for the training, setting up the room, and following up after the training.

IDENTIFY YOUR TRAINING NEEDS

To identify your training needs, answer this question: Why did you decide to conduct customer service training? Your immediate response might be "because we need it," but to answer this question reflectively you must first analyze and identify *what* needs to be improved, from both your business's and your employees' perspectives.

First, focus on your business. Make a list of your customer service training needs as they specifically relate to the type of products or services you provide, as well as your customers' needs. As you read through the book, relate the material to your business. For example, when reading the chapter on telephone contacts, you may have an "aha" moment and realize that your employees answer the phone in a nonprofessional manner.

Next, focus on your employees' needs. Make a customer service learning outcome list for each employee. Note strengths, areas of improvement, additional technical or job-skills training needed, and any behavioral issues (such as a poor attitude toward customers) that need to be addressed.

DEFINE LEARNING OUTCOMES

Review the needs you identified and develop a list of realistic learning outcomes. What skills should all your employees demonstrate at the end of the training session? It might help to note each chapter title and make a list of the skills in which your employees should be proficient.

Using the example of employees answering calls in a nonprofessional manner, one learning outcome for that chapter could be: Answer the telephone as ABC Company, then (employee's first name), then how may I help you? Listing specific outcomes before you begin training will enable you to measure how well your employees are using their new skills.

If you identified behavioral issues, you may want to make a separate list for those employees. This will help you focus on those items throughout the training sessions and follow up afterward.

PLAN YOUR TEACHING LESSONS

Create an introduction to kick off the training. Keep in mind that you will have everyone's undivided attention—during the first few minutes you're speaking! Use this to your advantage and develop a strong introduction. Keep it short, and stick to the basics. Explain why you are conducting this training and discuss general learning objectives. Then ask a question, tell a customer service story, or begin with a warm-up exercise or game. Use these first few minutes to grab your students' attention. As you work through each chapter (those applicable), try this approach:

- Begin each chapter by relating a positive personal experience where you were a customer (or ask for a student to volunteer) and that relates to the chapter material. For example, for Chapter 1, your example could be where you were a customer and formed a great first impression of an employee. Discuss the impact of the positive experience.

- Ask an open-ended question relevant to the example you cited. For example: *Why is it important to present yourself positively at all times?* Allow everyone to answer and discuss.

- Work through the material, step by step. Vary your delivery by reading out loud to the students, having them take turns reading out loud, or reading to themselves.

- Throughout each chapter, ask discussion questions related specifically to your business. For instance, *What are some things we should do to make a positive first impression?*

- After training each chapter, plan a group activity. Some suggestions:

  - Divide the group into teams. Assign a customer-related problem, dilemma, or question. Specify a time period to solve the problem. Each team will then present their solution to the group. Discuss the various solutions and choose the best one.

  - Divide the group into role-play pairs. Give each pair a customer service scenario and some additional details to help them get into their roles. For example, the customer is upset with your company, and the employee has a condescending attitude. Have one student play the role of the customer and another play the customer service employee. First, have students role-play the contact the wrong way; then do it again, role-playing the contact using the skills they are learning.

  - To energize the class, play a game related to the material. For example, after completing a session, have the group close their books and call out the key points for the chapter they have just completed. Toss a piece of candy to students as they answer correctly. Another option is to have a student call out an answer, then toss a ball to someone else who then must call out an answer.

  - Review and recap the key points. Have students complete the Practice Lesson and discuss answers.

  - Have students complete *How Do I Measure Up?* Encourage them to honestly analyze their skill levels.

ESTABLISH TIME FRAMES FOR TRAINING SESSIONS

Now that you have reviewed the training material and planned your lessons, you should be able to establish time frames. Think about your hours of operation, busy periods, and employee coverage. It is most effective, and probably easiest scheduling-wise, to cover the material in multiple sessions. This allows students to become comfortable with the material learned in each chapter.

When scheduling your classes, add a little extra time to your estimate to make sure your students will not feel rushed. Write a schedule to which you can conform. You will lose credibility with your employees if you schedule a class and then cancel. Give your training sessions top priority. If you demonstrate that customer service training is important to you, learning customer service skills will be important to your employees.

PREPARE YOURSELF FOR THE TRAINING

When you train, establish an open and relaxed atmosphere that encourages discussion by maintaining a positive attitude, keeping focused, remaining upbeat, staying energized, encouraging everyone to participate, and focusing on the end goals.

Rehearse and practice your presentations—both the general introduction and how you plan to handle each chapter. It is perfectly normal to feel nervous, particularly if training is not part of your routine responsibilities. Being well prepared will help you manage your nerves. Practice may not make perfect, but it will help you gain confidence and feel more assured. Here are some tips for training others:

- Focus on your students rather than on yourself.

- Keep in mind the importance of the material.

- Stay on track by making good notes—and using them.

- Try to stick to the allotted time, but be sure you plan enough time to be thorough. Do not rush against a time clock. It is better to adjust the time than the material.

- When you speak, make eye contact with your students, switching your gaze from one person to another at a pace that is comfortable, not staged.

■ Vary your voice tone and inflection.

■ Be yourself.

■ If you become nervous, take slow, deep breaths to calm yourself.

SET UP THE ROOM

Plan a setting that is conducive to training. First, find a suitable room or area that is free from distractions and noise. For a small group, a U-shaped, rectangular, or round table works well. This way all the students can face each other for discussions, and you will be able to move easily within and around the group. If you will be using an easel or whiteboard for discussion answers, place it so that all students can see it.

Think of ways to energize your students. Look for signs of tiredness or boredom—yawning, fidgeting, or a glazed-over look. Here are some tips for energizing your group:

■ Schedule short breaks every hour or two.

■ Lead frequent stand-up-and-stretch and deep-breathing exercises.

■ Vary the class activities.

■ Keep the class interactive by incorporating frequent discussions and other activities.

FOLLOW UP AFTER THE TRAINING

Spend time with your employees to observe their customer contacts. Try to catch them "doing it right." When you do, acknowledge good performance by giving feedback that is specific to the behavior you observed. Rather than saying "you did a great job," be more specific by saying "I really liked the way you handled Mrs. Johnson when she was upset. The way you explained our delivery schedule was right on target and you made sure she understood completely." Now your employee knows exactly what was done right, and the behavior is more apt to be repeated.

It can be a great motivator to praise an employee within earshot of other employees, but it is never acceptable to discuss poor performance in public. When you hear an employee handling a customer poorly, take that employee aside to discuss the incident.

Recognize your group's efforts by commending them, by awarding total team efforts, and by reading customer commendations at meetings.

Most important, be consistent with your team. Recognizing good behavior yesterday but ignoring it today will confuse your employees. Make sure customer service is important to you every day; then it will be important to your employees every day as well.

Tips for the Student

Why is customer service training important? The answer is simple: Treating your customers well is essential to your company and to your job. Learning how to give exceptional customer service is necessary for any business to succeed. Customers have many choices. If they are not happy with the way they are treated, they can take their business elsewhere. Always remember:

CUSTOMERS ARE THE REASON YOU HAVE A JOB

Whether your manager purchased this book for a training class or you purchased it to improve your own skills, you are going to learn how to present yourself well and how to handle different types of customers in varying situations.

Before you begin your training classes or read the book, it will be beneficial to identify your personal needs and define learning outcomes. This will help you prepare for learning new skills, enable you to get the most out of the material, and help you self-monitor after training.

IDENTIFY YOUR PERSONAL NEEDS AND DEFINE LEARNING OUTCOMES

Think about your typical customer contacts. Which types of customers or customer interactions are you uncomfortable handling? For example, are you unsure how to talk to customers who are upset and confront you in an angry tone? Make a list of any areas in which you need improvement or guidance.

Now think about your job from a technical standpoint. What must you learn to do your job effectively? Make a list of those areas in which you need additional training. Before you begin your customer service training, give this list to your manager and ask for the technical training you need. You must feel comfortable with your products, services, and policies before you can feel comfortable helping each customer.

Finally, think about what you want to gain from training. Make a list of learning outcomes. Turn your areas of improvement into learning outcomes by rephrasing them as positive statements. For example, not knowing how to deal with customers who are angry could be written as a learning objective: turn angry customers into satisfied ones.

PREPARE FOR THE TRAINING SESSION

Whether you are a student in a class or working through the material on your own, reading and learning puts you into a different routine. When you are used to working with customers and coworkers, staying alert when you sit, read, and work through a book can be difficult. Make the most of the training sessions by:

- Getting enough sleep the night before training

- Eating a healthy breakfast

- Knowing what to expect during the class

- Taking deep breaths when you feel drowsy

- Standing and stretching when you feel sleepy

- Taking a short walking break when you feel ready to nod off

GET THE MOST OUT OF THE MATERIAL

As you work through each chapter, relate what you are reading to the type of customer interactions you handle. You may choose to focus on a specific customer scenario for each chapter. If you do, use the blank pages found in Part II to write down a typical customer request. You can refer to this scenario when answering the Practice Lesson questions.

Each chapter follows a similar format:

- General chapter information

- "The Wrong Way To ___"

- Overview of the key points that will be covered in the chapter

- Next, each key point is explained step-by-step in an in-depth manner, followed by "The Right Way To _____."

- Business "Not" as Usual

- Summary of key points and steps

- Practice Lesson

- Doing It Right!

- How Do I Measure Up?

In addition, each chapter contains handy tips and discussion topics for group-meeting brainstorming sessions.

TIP   BRAINSTORM   BUSINESS **NØT** AS USUAL

If you are learning on your own, read through a chapter, then review the key points and steps. If you feel comfortable with the material, work the Practice Lesson. If you are not comfortable, go back over the chapter. Make sure you understand the material before moving on. Give yourself time to practice the steps in each chapter before moving on to the next.

SELF-MONITOR AFTER TRAINING

Review your list of learning outcomes. Do you feel comfortable that you have mastered each? If not, review the relevant chapters again. Then, if you still feel uncomfortable or unsure, talk to your manager so together you can turn your areas of improvement into strengths.

Most important, enjoy the work you do. Your customers and co-workers depend on you to be your best.

I

PUTTING YOUR
BEST FACE FORWARD

Your First Steps Can Make a Huge Stride: The Basics

**WHATEVER BUSINESS YOU ARE IN,
THE CUSTOMER IS THE REASON YOU HAVE A JOB**

You may be wondering what has happened to customer service. Think, for a moment, about your own interactions as a customer. In the past few days, how many times were you a customer? Did you go to the grocery store or the mall? Did you visit the post office, doctor's office, bank, dry cleaners, or your child's school? Did you eat any meals out? Did you call a company to ask a question or shop online?

You probably were a customer more times than you realized. As a customer, you have choices. How many stores are in your mall? How many doctors are in your phone book? How many restaurants are nearby? And if you shop online, you know the choices are endless. In your interactions, how many times were you met with boredom, indifference, rudeness, or condescension? How many times were you greeted with a friendly smile and an enthusiastic attitude? Did this enthusiastic attitude come as a surprise, and were you thrilled or even grateful for the experience? Customers should never have to feel grateful for being treated well. Being treated well should be the standard.

The reality is that if you are not happy with the service at one business, you have the option of going elsewhere. When you are given great service, you are likely to go back for repeat business. You are also likely to recommend the business to your friends. As a service provider, keep in mind that your customers have the same choices you do. How you treat your customers does matter. If they are not happy with the way you treat them, they can, and probably will, go elsewhere.

Think again about your own interactions as a customer. Which ones stand out in your mind? You will remember service that is outstanding or awful. Mediocre service is soon forgotten. Be someone who is remembered for being outstanding.

CUSTOMER SERVICE IS THE BASICS

We are going to take our first steps with the basics because:

The basics are the basis of customer service.

A favorable first impression is the basis of customer service. You begin providing service the moment you respond to a customer who comes into your business, calls you on the telephone, emails you, or posts on social media. When customers physically walk through your door, they take a mental snapshot of you and your surroundings. Without even thinking about it, they form a first impression. First impressions are also formed over the telephone and through online contact. How you speak, how well you listen, the words you choose, and how you write and respond all contribute to first impressions. If a customer's first impression is favorable, you have laid the foundation for providing great customer service. If the first impression is not favorable, you will have to dig deeper to begin building your foundation.

Being courteous is the basis of customer service. Customers appreciate courteous treatment. As young children, we learned basic courtesies: to say "please" and "thank you"; to pay attention and not to interrupt when other people speak; to treat others with respect; to play fairly; to say "I'm sorry." As adults, we sometimes forget how important these words and actions are. Courtesy words, phrases, and behaviors contain powerful messages. They show that you care.

A positive attitude is the basis of customer service. Customers appreciate a positive attitude. A great attitude can help overcome a poor first impression. Similarly, a negative attitude can destroy a favorable first impression.

Being truthful and acting in an ethical manner is the basis of customer service. Honesty is always the best policy. When you follow through on commitments and stay accountable for your actions, you show your customers that you value them and that they can rely on you to do the right thing.

By combining a favorable first impression, courteous treatment, a positive attitude, and ethical behaviors, you build a strong customer service foundation. Add effective communication skills, and you will be on your way to establishing long-lasting relationships with your customers. Once you master these customer service basics, learn how to effectively communicate, and develop skills to build strong relationships, you will confidently handle any customer in any situation.

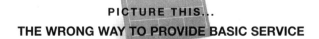

PICTURE THIS...
THE WRONG WAY TO PROVIDE BASIC SERVICE

Sally drove to Bob's Electronic Store to look for a new television set. She walked in and spotted two employees stocking streaming devices on a display rack. They were laughing and joking with each other as they

worked. Neither looked at her. Neither asked if she needed help.
She asked where she could find television sets. Without looking up,
one of the employees said, "They're over there," pointing as he answered.
She wandered over to the television sets. With so many different models
from which to choose, she was confused and did not know which would
be best for her needs. She noticed the employees were still joking around.
Sally waited a few moments and, when neither one paid attention to her,
she walked out of the store.

What Went Wrong?

Sally did not form a favorable first impression of the employees at
Bob's Electronic Store. Neither stopped what they were doing to help
her. Neither was courteous. They could have changed her first impression
by projecting an attitude that they cared about her as a customer and
by taking the time to talk with her and help her.

How Did the Customer Feel?

Sally was dissatisfied with the way she was treated. It appeared to her
that the employees felt that stocking shelves and talking to each other
were more important than helping her. Sally felt that her business simply
did not matter to Bob's employees. Since she did not care for the way
she was treated, Sally left without doing business with them.

When you work with customers continuously, it is easy to begin taking them for granted. Taking customers for granted is never acceptable. When you do, you stop caring about how you treat them. Eventually, you may view customers as though they are intruders who take you away from your work. This was the view Bob's employees projected. To them, stocking shelves and talking to each other were more important. When you do not treat your customers well, you may soon find you do not have many customers to help.

Customers have been conditioned to expect mediocre service and, when they are given mediocre service, they will have mediocre attitudes about the business. When customers are valued and treated with courtesy and respect, they are more apt to do repeat business with you. Remember the important lesson you learned as a child: Always treat others the way you want to be treated. Treat others well, and they are more likely to treat you well.

Mastering the basics is simple once you learn and practice the four steps below. Then you will begin to build a firm foundation for providing great customer service.

Step 1: First Impressions Matter

Step 2: Courtesy Counts

Step 3: Attitude Is Everything

Step 4: Doing the Right Thing: Ethical Issues

If Bob's employees had treated Sally better, she would not have walked out of the store. She left because they did not value her as a customer. They did not lay the basic foundation for giving great customer service.

STEP 1
FIRST IMPRESSIONS MATTER

The moment customers see you or speak to you, they begin forming their impressions of you. First impressions are mental snapshots you take when you first encounter a person or situation. They include a person's looks and actions: general grooming and cleanliness, clothing, voice tone, attitude, and body language. First impressions matter; yet even when you present yourself well, customers may not form a positive impression because of preconceived ideas or biases. In those situations, you can change a person's impression by speaking courteously and projecting a positive attitude.

When Sally took her mental snapshot at Bob's, it did not develop well. Even if the employees were well-dressed and groomed, their lack of courtesy and poor attitudes spoke volumes. When they ignored Sally, they told her loudly and clearly that they did not value her as a customer.

Appearance Is the First Thing Customers Notice About You

The first step to making a good first impression is your appearance. When you do not have an appealing appearance, you can present an obstacle that blocks your customers from forming a positive first impression. You do not have to sacrifice your personal style to please others, but when you are at work you do need to make sure your appearance is fitting for your business. If you don't, you may have to work harder for your customers to feel comfortable with you.

Wear Appropriate Clothing for the Type of Work You Do

Wear the type of clothing that fits the character of your business. If you work in a fine dining restaurant, you will dress quite differently than if you work in a fast-food restaurant. When in doubt about what type clothing is suitable for your job, always lean toward dressing conservatively. Save your party clothes for parties. Save your torn jeans and old tees for hanging out with friends. No matter what type of clothes you wear to work, you do not have to spend a fortune on your wardrobe. Wearing well-fitted and suitable clothes will go a long way toward presenting yourself appropriately. It does not matter how much you spend; what matters most is how your clothes fit you and your environment.

Make Sure You Are Groomed

Being groomed means your hair and fingernails are clean and neat; your face, body, and teeth are clean; your clothes are clean and pressed; your shoes are in good repair; your hair is styled; and your overall image is professional. Put all that together, and you present a groomed look.

TIP

If you do not have a full-length mirror, buy one. Look in it every day before you leave home.

Present Positive Body Language

You can wear nice clothes, be clean and groomed, yet still convey a negative first impression if you slouch, yawn, look bored, or have a scowl on your face. Body language includes your demeanor, facial expressions, and eye contact. Your body language may even be more important than your appearance, because it conveys your inner feelings and emotions. Whether you present an angry, bored, or friendly demeanor, it shows.

Hold your head high, and stand or sit up straight. When standing, keep your arms relaxed naturally at your sides or with hands folded in front of you. Keep your facial expressions friendly and make eye contact when customers come into your business. Smile as often as appropriate. A smile goes a long way in presenting a positive image. When you smile, you will not only make the other person feel better, you will feel better yourself.

TIP

Tone of voice, listening skills, speaking skills, and writing skills all contribute to the first impressions customers form when they are not in a face-to-face situation. Smile when you answer the phone. When speaking or writing, choose positive and enthusiastic words, like "I'll be happy to help you." Even if the customer voices a complaint, your words should convey assurance. "I'm sorry that happened. I'll check on that right away for you."

Taking these steps will help your customers begin to form a positive first impression of you.

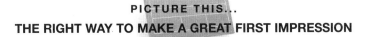

PICTURE THIS...
THE RIGHT WAY TO MAKE A GREAT FIRST IMPRESSION

Sally drove to Bob's Electronic Store to purchase a new television set. She walked in and spotted two employees stocking streaming devices on a display rack. They were dressed nicely and looked happy, laughing and joking with each other while they worked. They looked at her, smiled, and said "Welcome to Bob's." The employees were well-groomed, and their body language conveyed the message that they cared about themselves. Their smiles conveyed the message that they cared about her. Sally smiled back and said she was looking for a new television.

How Did the Customer Feel?

This time Sally's mental snapshot was developing nicely. The employees made a great first impression because they stopped what they were doing to greet her.

STEP 2
COURTESY COUNTS

Basic courtesies are the words you say and the manners you display to show consideration, politeness, and respect toward others. But the fact is that we live in such a fast-paced world that people are often in too much of a hurry to be courteous. But even though you cannot control how your customers treat you, you can control how you treat them. When you treat others courteously, they are likely to treat you the same way. Treating others with courtesy and good manners may even change someone's bad behavior!

Customers continue forming their first impression when you begin to interact with them. If a customer's first impression was favorable, displaying basic courtesies will enhance the customer's perception; and in the event the customer did not form a positive first impression, you can turn that around by speaking and acting with respect and using good manners.

Basic courtesies include both the words you choose and the actions you take. When you act courteously, you send a positive and powerful message. When you make a conscious effort to use courteous words and phrases, they will soon become a natural part of your vocabulary and personality.

Say Please, Thank You, and You're Welcome

We were taught these words as young children, and we were taught these words for a reason: They are an important part of communication because they convey caring and respect. As a child, you were likely prompted to use these words. "What do you say?" was your prompt to respond with "please," or "thank you," or "you're welcome." Pay attention to your internal prompts. Make it a habit to incorporate these words into your vocabulary and use them frequently.

Say Excuse Me and I'm Sorry

Growing up, you learned that when you did not understand someone, when someone was in your way, or when you inadvertently did something incorrectly, you said "excuse me." When you did something wrong or made a mistake, you learned to say "I'm sorry." Saying "I'm sorry" can be particularly difficult for adults. Get in the habit of adding this to your vocabulary. The next time you do something wrong, say "I'm sorry." Not only will you make the other person feel better, *you* will feel better. These two words go a long way in repairing relationship damage. There are occasions when an apology goes a long way even when you did not do something wrong, for example "I'm so sorry that happened": In this instance, you are not accepting blame, but rather displaying compassion.

Use Sir and Ma'am

Using these words shows a sign of respect. When you call a person sir or ma'am, be careful how you accentuate these words. The wrong emphasis can make you sound sarcastic or condescending. The right emphasis can make you sound respectful, no matter your age, no matter your customer's age.

Use a Person's Name When You Know It

Everyone enjoys hearing his or her name, so if you know your customer's name use it. Addressing a customer by name adds a personal touch to your interaction. Address a customer by first name only if you feel the customer is comfortable with that. Also, be sure to always give the customer your name.

Use Yes Rather Than Yeah

"Yes" sounds professional, intelligent, and respectful. Period. Save "yeah" for informal personal conversations. Better yet, get into the habit of always using "yes."

Always Behave in a Courteous Manner

Wait for the other person to finish speaking before you speak. Shake hands when you are introduced to someone. Keep your work space neat and orderly, especially when customers are present. Hold the door open for the next person. Allow someone to go ahead of you. When you make it a daily goal to act courteously, it will become second nature.

Say It with a Smile

This is an old saying with a timely meaning. When you smile at someone, they usually smile back. Smiling when you speak comes across loud and clear. Whether you are speaking face to face or by telephone, your customers will see or hear the smile in your voice.

TIP

Common courtesies also include negative things, you should not do in the presence of customers: talking on a personal call, texting or staring at your phone, smoking, eating (or having food at your workstation), and chewing gum.

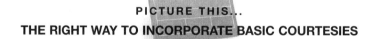

PICTURE THIS...
THE RIGHT WAY TO INCORPORATE BASIC COURTESIES

Sally smiled back at the two employees and said "I'm looking for a new television, but there are so many new types I really don't know what I'm looking for. Can you help me?"

"Yes, Ma'am. My name is Jeff, and I'll be happy to help you," said one of the employees as he smiled warmly and walked toward her. "Let me show you what we have." He walked with her to the television sets.

How Did the Customer Feel?

Jeff was courteous and Sally felt that he truly cared about helping her.

STEP 3
ATTITUDE IS EVERYTHING

People may not remember the color of your shirt or the exact words you said, but they will remember your attitude. Your attitude is the "face" you present to the world. Your feelings, emotions, and beliefs about yourself and others are reflected outward through your attitude. Projecting a positive attitude is another way to make a good—and long-lasting—impression on others. Positive attitudes rub off. When you are positive, you can uplift others.

Attitude Is Everything—Good or Bad

Whether yours is good or bad, your attitude is what people are going to remember about you. When you interact with customers, you may not get a second chance. Even if you are not a naturally upbeat person, you can train yourself to have a more positive attitude. When you wake every morning, you have a choice about your attitude. Make the choice to make a positive difference.

Appreciate the Good in Yourself and in Others

Appreciation can be learned by changing your self-talk (the words you use when you think) to positive thoughts. This goes for thoughts about yourself. Change "I'll never do this right" to "Next time, I'll do better." This also goes for thoughts about your customers: "This old lady is really dumb. She doesn't have a clue about television sets. This is going to be a tough one." Change this mindset to "I'll do what I can to help her. She doesn't know a lot about the new technology, so I'll do my best to explain everything." Changing your self-talk helps you appreciate yourself and others. When you find yourself falling into old habits of negative self-talk, make a conscious effort to change your thought process.

Believe in Yourself

When you stop your negative self-talk, you will start to believe in yourself. Saying things such as "I'll never do this right" sets you up for failure. Changing your self-talk to "Next time, I'll remember the correct way" sets you up for success. Be kind to yourself and choose constructive and respectful self-talk. When you begin to believe in yourself, you will begin to feel more confident. When you feel more confident, you will begin projecting a positive image to others. To your customers, you will project an image of someone who believes in yourself, your company, and your products.

Believe You Can Make a Difference

As your confidence grows, you will feel a sense of purpose and you will want to make a difference in the lives of others. Helping someone gives a great sense of helpfulness and accomplishment. When you believe you can make a difference, you will find ways to make it happen. Pay attention and stay tuned in. Listen closely to what your customer is saying. Stay engaged to ensure your understanding. Do all you can to help each customer. When you do these things, you will make a positive difference.

Keep an Open Mind; Do Not Stereotype People

Stereotyping others who may be different from you can often be skewed, biased, and negative. When the employee thought about the older woman who did not know what she wanted and was going to be tough to deal with, he was accepting a negative stereotype about her before he had even talked to her. When you change your thought process and stop stereotyping others, you will change the way you present yourself. Train yourself to practice tolerance toward others who are different from you. Accept that people are different and accept others for who they are.

Maintain Your Positive Attitude

Negative circumstances can easily zap anyone's positive attitude. If someone has upset you or if you find yourself feeling stressed, try to get away from the situation for a few minutes. Getting away will not only help you calm down, it will give you time to think through the situation and put things in perspective. The best way to maintain a positive attitude is to take care of yourself every day. Get enough rest. Exercise your body and mind. Eat healthful foods. Do something fun. Do something just for you. When you do these things every day, you will find it easier to stay upbeat and positive.

TIP

We all carry emotional baggage. When you arrive at work, leave your emotional baggage at the door. Never make your customers and coworkers suffer because you are having a problem. Remember that everyone has problems. Use your work time to focus on your customers and your work.

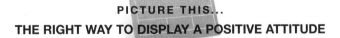

PICTURE THIS...
THE RIGHT WAY TO DISPLAY A POSITIVE ATTITUDE

As they walked to the television sets, Jeff asked "Have you been to Bob's before?" When Sally shook her head, he smiled and continued enthusiastically, "I'm glad you came in. Not only do we offer the lowest prices around, we stand behind all our merchandise."

Sally nodded. She felt comfortable that Jeff truly wanted to help her. When they reached the television display, Jeff said "I'll tell you about the different types of sets we have and be happy to answer any questions." He took the time to answer all her questions and guided her to make the right choice.

How Did the Customer Feel?

Sally completed developing her mental snapshot. Because she appreciated Jeff's confident, positive attitude, Sally trusted him to give her good suggestions.

STEP 4
DOING THE RIGHT THING: ETHICAL ISSUES

The last step of customer service basics deals with ethics. Being ethical means being honest and truthful, doing the right thing, and being accountable for your actions. When you make the commitment to be honest and do the right thing for all your customers, you will act ethically and treat every customer fairly. Customers appreciate fair treatment, and they have the good sense to know when they are not being treated fairly. Acting ethically means that sometimes you will need to make tough decisions rather than taking the easy way out.

Always Be Honest

Being honest at all times will make your life far less complicated. When you are truthful, you do not have to remember what you said to whom. Being truthful is important to your customers. When you are dishonest, people find out. Maybe not right away, but the truth always has a way of coming out. When people find out you have not been completely honest, they will no longer trust you.

Always Be Truthful About Your Products, Services, and Policies

Never make misleading claims or comment negatively about your competitors. If a customer asks for a comparison or leads you to say something negative, say "I don't know about that, but let me explain our policy. . . ." or "I don't know enough about that to comment. Let me explain how our product works and why I feel it's best for you."

Do the Right Thing

Doing the right thing means thinking through your course of action before you take it. It means taking the high road even when that means opting for a tough solution. Doing the right thing means treating each customer equitably. When you make the decision to do the right thing for others, you will go out of your way to do your best. When you are faced with a dilemma, always base your decision on doing what is right and ethical.

Do What You Say You Will When You Say You Will

Ethical behavior means that your words match your actions. Saying one thing but doing another causes people to lose trust. Following through on what you say conveys that you are dependable and trustworthy. Become a person on whom others can rely. When you give a customer your word, mean it. Let your word be your bond. Erase the words "I can't" and "no" from your vocabulary. If you cannot do what the customer asks, explain instead what you can do. It is all right to say "I don't know." Just be sure to follow up with "I'll find out for you."

Stay Accountable for Your Actions

Staying accountable will keep you on the right path and enable you to act ethically in all situations. Ethical people hold themselves accountable for their actions and take responsibility for their mistakes. You are human; therefore you are going to make mistakes. What is important is what you do after you make a mistake. If you think you have done something incorrect or unethical, be up front and talk it over with your manager. Ask what you can do to make things right. Then make it right. Apologize if you have wronged someone.

When you take responsibility and own up to your mistakes, people will respect you. Owning up to a mistake may not be easy at first, but it is the right thing to do. People will appreciate that you are able to admit you did something wrong. You will also have an added benefit: You will respect yourself more when you take responsibility for your actions.

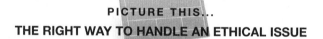

PICTURE THIS...
THE RIGHT WAY TO HANDLE AN ETHICAL ISSUE

Sally was ready to buy. She said, "I heard that JB Appliances gives you a wireless speaker when you purchase a television. I'll buy from you if you match that offer."

Jeff was not familiar with JB's policy. Before he answered, he thought about what to say. He could have said, "JB offers that because they sell their televisions at a higher price, and they don't stand behind their merchandise. I've heard complaints about them." Or he might have said, "Well, we usually don't do that, but for you I'll make an exception."

Here is how Jeff answered Sally: "I'm not familiar with what JB Appliances offers, but here's what we offer. We keep our merchandise priced low to consistently give our customers the best deal. And we stand behind our products."

By positively reassuring Sally and explaining their policy, Jeff did not get involved in an ethical dilemma. Sally left Bob's with a new television set.

How Did the Customer Feel?

Sally bought her television set at Bob's because she felt that Jeff's honest and ethical response meant more than getting something for free.

Do you know what is considered ethical and, more important, what is considered unethical, in your business? If you are unclear, discuss specific situations that may be construed as unethical. Every employee should be completely certain that they know the difference. Even when you do understand your ethics policies, you may find yourself in a position in which you mishandle a situation. Let's say that one of your customers asks you to do something special or unusual, such as waiving a service fee. In order to make the sale, you comply but later realize that you crossed ethical boundaries. How do you handle the situation? Do you call the customer and retract the favor? Do you extend the favor to all customers, having done it for one?

In a group, discuss how to handle sticky situations you may encounter. Then come up with suggested responses. Role-play to reinforce ethical behavior.

PICTURE THIS...
PUTTING IT ALL TOGETHER

Sally drove to Bob's Electronic Store to purchase a new television set. She walked in and spotted two employees stocking streaming devices on a display rack. They were dressed nicely and looked happy, as they laughed and joked with each other while they worked. They looked at her, smiled, and said "Welcome to Bob's." The employees were well-groomed, and their body language conveyed the message that they cared about themselves. Their smiles conveyed the message that they cared about her.

Sally smiled back and said "I'm looking for a new television, but there are so many new types that I really don't know what I'm looking for. Can you help me?"

"Yes, Ma'am. My name is Jeff, and I'll be happy to help you," said one of the employees as he smiled warmly and walked toward her. "Let me show you what we have." He walked with her to the television sets.

Jeff asked "Have you been to Bob's before?" When Sally shook her head, he smiled and continued enthusiastically, "I'm glad you came in. Not only do we offer the lowest prices around, we stand behind all our merchandise."

Sally nodded. She felt comfortable that Jeff truly wanted to help her.

When they reached the television display, Jeff said "I'll tell you about the different types of sets we have, and I am happy to answer any questions." He took the time to answer all her questions and guided her to make the right choice.

Sally was ready to buy. She said "I heard that JB Appliances gives you a wireless speaker when you purchase a television. I'll buy from you if you match that offer."

Jeff answered "I'm not familiar with what JB Appliances offers, but here's what we offer. We keep our merchandise priced low to consistently give our customers the best deal. And we stand behind our products."

By positively reassuring Sally and explaining their policy, Jeff did not get involved in an ethical dilemma. Sally left Bob's with a new television set.

Customer service begins when take your first steps by making a great first impression, being courteous, displaying a positive attitude, and being truthful and ethical with your customers. It really is that simple.

**BUSINESS
NØT
AS USUAL**

Whatever Business You Are in, the Customer Is the Reason You Have a Job

Think about the truth in these words. It is always important to appreciate your customers. In today's business world with so much competition, customers have numerous options. Showing appreciation to each and every one of your customers takes on a more literal meaning. Consider that each customer who comes into your business may well be the one responsible for your job. So:

- Make a positive first impression.

- Be helpful and enthusiastic.

- Keep your facial expressions friendly.

- Say it with a smile.

- Do everything with integrity.

- Never give the customer a reason to lose trust in your company.

- Attitude is everything—make sure yours is positive.

K E Y   P O I N T S

Step 1: First Impressions Matter

- Appearance is the first thing people notice about you.

- Wear appropriate clothing for the type of work you do.

- Make sure you are well groomed.

- Present positive body language.

Step 2: Courtesy Counts

- Say "please," "thank you," and "you're welcome."

- Say "excuse me" and "I'm sorry."

- Use "sir" and "ma'am."

- Use a person's name when you know it.

- Use "yes" rather than "yeah."

- Say it with a smile.

Step 3: Attitude Is Everything

- Attitude is everything—good or bad.

- Appreciate the good in yourself and in others.

- Believe in yourself.

- Believe you can make a difference.

- Keep an open mind; do not stereotype people.

Step 4: Doing the Right Thing: Ethical Issues

- Always be honest.

- Do the right thing.

- Do what you say you will when you say you will.

- Be accountable for your actions.

PRACTICE LESSON

Step 1: First Impressions Matter

Write down some things you can do to make a good first impression.

_____

_____

Step 2: Courtesy Counts

Write some statements you can say to your customers that incorporate basic courtesies.

_____

_____

Step 3: Attitude Is Everything

What are some things you can do to present a great attitude?

_____

_____

Step 4: Doing the Right Thing: Ethical Issues

Think of a situation in which a customer asks you to do something unethical. Briefly describe the situation and your response to the customer.

_____

_____

D O I N G   I T   R I G H T !

John works part-time in a tire store. He is attending technical college, training to be an auto technician. To some, this would be "just a job," a stepping-stone to a better career. Yet, even though John earns little more than the minimum wage, he treats this job as though it is the best job in the world. Every day, he gives his customers, his boss, and his coworkers his all.

I was fortunate to walk into this tire store on a day when John was working. He looked directly at me, smiled, and greeted me warmly. "Hi, welcome to Westview Tire," he called out enthusiastically. "How can I help you today?" His "take-charge" demeanor and outgoing personality told me loud and clear that I mattered. Upon meeting him, I knew I was in good hands.

After he made this great first impression, I noticed that John frequently incorporated courtesy words and phrases into his vocabulary. He respectfully answered "Yes, Ma'am," or "No, Ma'am." His upbeat attitude was refreshing.

His enthusiasm was contagious, and I couldn't help but smile as he fully explained the different tires he had in stock and then recommended what he felt would be the best choice for me. My mental snapshot was developing nicely. He was knowledgeable and made sure he answered my questions thoroughly. Here is this young man, a student working part-time in a tire store earning not much more than minimum wage, fully engaged in his work and his customers.

I commended John to his boss, who smiled broadly. He told me he knew how lucky he was to have hired John, commenting that "John's friendliness and his direct, honest approach usually develops into long-lasting relationships."

I asked John how he managed to stay so positive. His answer was great: "I appreciate this job, my boss, and my customers. I try to treat everyone the way I want to be treated."

When commenting on his ability to make a great first impression, John replied "I always try my best to make a good first impression. After all, you never know who you're impressing!"

True words!

H O W   D O   I   M E A S U R E   U P ?

1. What first impression am I making with my customers?

   _____

   _____

2. What courtesy words and phrases am I remembering to use? Which ones do I need to remember to use?

   _____

   _____

3. How well am I maintaining a positive attitude? What are my "negative" triggers and what can I do to stay upbeat and positive?

   _____

   _____

4. How honest and ethical am I? Am I doing the right thing in all situations? If not, what can I do to correct these behaviors?

   _____

   _____

2

Tossing the Ball Back and Forth: Effective Communication

**EFFECTIVE COMMUNICATION IS THE FIRM FOUNDATION
UPON WHICH YOU BUILD STRONG RELATIONSHIPS**

Did you know that almost everything you do involves some form of communication? Even when you are not actively vocalizing a message, you communicate. When you smile at a stranger, hold a door open for the person behind you, nod as a sign of thank you, or listen attentively when someone is talking to you, you communicate. You even communicate by doing nothing at all. When you ignore someone, stare at your phone when someone is talking, let a door close on the person behind you, or look the other way when someone is approaching, you communicate.

Communication styles change, often subconsciously, depending on the person or the situation. You communicate one way with your children, another way with your friends, and yet another way with your customers. You may take an authoritative, a deferential, or an equal role. At work, your customers likely view you as an authority figure to help them. You can enhance the first impressions your customers form by the way in which you speak to them. When a customer comes into your place of business and you smile and offer a warm greeting, you communicate a positive message. When you answer a call and speak courteously, you communicate a positive message. When you respond quickly to a social media query, you communicate a positive message.

CUSTOMER SERVICE IS EFFECTIVE COMMUNICATION

As a frontline employee, you are your customers' point of contact and their primary communication source. To them, you not only represent the company, you *are* the company.

Therefore, you are your company's chief communicator. Presenting yourself well has a direct bearing on a customer's perception of your ability to handle the interaction satisfactorily.

In fact, presenting yourself well is your most important job. Relationships develop when effective communication is established. You will learn about building relationships in Chapter 3, but first you will learn valuable communication skills. Communication forms the basis of any relationship; learning how to communicate effectively is imperative when you deal with customers. In this chapter, we focus on verbal and nonverbal communication.

The easiest way to communicate is when you are face to face with people, because you have the advantage of being able to pick up cues about a person's mood and can adjust your conversation accordingly. You do not have that advantage when communicating by phone, so your voice tone is an important communication tool. You may have the best advantage through written communication because you can read—and change—what you write before sending. When speaking face to face or by phone, you have no backspace or delete key to change your message, so it is vital that you say exactly what you mean to say.

You also communicate without saying a word. Whether communicating face to face or by phone, your nonverbal signals account for a major portion of communication. Nonverbal communication includes your body language, facial expressions, eye movements, gestures, and voice tone. You may say one thing but communicate something completely different. Words communicate a message; nonverbal signals communicate the emotions behind the message.

Try this nonverbal exercise: Picture yourself explaining a company policy to a customer. As you are speaking:

Look at the person and smile.

Slump over and yawn.

Lower your eyes to the floor.

Stand with your arms crossed in front of you.

When you look directly at someone and smile, you convey interest. When you slump and yawn, you convey boredom. When you lower your eyes to the floor, you convey disinterest or dishonesty. When you stand with your arms crossed in front of you, you build an imaginary wall between yourself and the other person. You can say the right words but still convey the wrong message.

Now try this voice tone exercise: Ask the following question out loud in an enthusiastic tone:

"Can I help you?"

Now repeat it in:

An uncertain tone

A condescending tone

A disinterested tone

Notice how the same four words take on four very different meanings, depending on your voice tone. *How* you say something is even more important than the words you choose. How you say something can help—or hinder—the effectiveness of your communication.

As your company's chief communicator, it is also important that what you are saying is being interpreted the way you mean it; otherwise, the message may be taken the wrong way. When that happens, it takes more of your time and energy to correct the listener's interpretation of your meaning, and you may even lose the customer. When you speak, it is important that you choose your words carefully and use good grammar, which helps communicate the correct message.

A large part of your communication with customers is asking questions. Knowing what questions to ask is crucial, but also crucial is knowing when and how to ask them. Another large part of your communication with customers is answering questions. Knowing your products and services helps, but so does your ability to speak effectively. When you ask questions to find the right solutions, you may receive objections to your proposals. Learning how to handle objections is important in being able to provide each customer with the best solution.

Listening, though covered last, is the most important part of communication because it is the critical component for understanding. Unless you listen completely and attentively, you may respond incorrectly or improperly. Sometimes it is difficult to listen well because of distractions. Overcoming barriers that make listening difficult will increase your ability to stay focused. Employing nonverbal listening strategies can also enhance your ability to demonstrate that you are both listening and understanding.

PICTURE THIS...
THE WRONG WAY TO COMMUNICATE EFFECTIVELY

Steve stopped at the local deli for lunch. He was in a hurry to place the order for himself and his coworkers, and he was greeted by an employee who yawned as he looked at Steve. Scratching his head with his pencil, he said "Hey man, whaddyawant?"

Steve began to give his order: "I'll have a turkey and Swiss on whole wheat with mayo and tomatoes. . . ." As he spoke, he noticed that the employee kept looking at the door whenever someone came in. Steve finished his order, "a ham on rye with mustard, and a pastrami on rye with mustard."

The employee said "Okay, a ham on rye and a pastrami on rye. What do you want on 'em?"

As Steve answered "mustard" in an annoyed tone, he wondered if the employee had gotten the rest of the order. "Did you get the turkey and Swiss, the roast beef, and the tuna salad?"

Without looking up, the employee said "Yeah" in an agitated voice.

Steve said: "I'm in a hurry. How long do you think it'll take?"

The employee shrugged nonchalantly. "It shouldn't take long." He strolled slowly to the back room with Steve's order.

Before Steve left, he checked his order because he was not certain the employee had gotten it right.

What Went Wrong?

The employee looked tired, bored, and was more interested in seeing who was coming in than in helping Steve. His lack of attention, poor choice of words, and lazy grammar did nothing to help Steve feel confident that the order would be right.

How Did the Customer Feel?

Because the employee paid more attention to who was coming and going, Steve had no confidence that the employee had gotten the order correctly.

He felt that the employee did not care about him as a customer and wondered if the owner/manager cared about the way the employees handled customers.

Effective communication is always important. Where you work does not matter: When your primary job is to be your company's chief communicator, you project your company's image to your customers. By learning the six steps that follow, you will learn valuable tools that will help you to become a more effective communicator.

Step 1: Say What You Mean and Mean What You Say

Step 2: Enhance Your Messages with Nonverbal Techniques

Step 3: Putting Words Together: Grammar Usage

Step 4: Ask the Correct Questions and Answer the Questions Correctly

Step 5: Overcome the Big No

Step 6: Listen Attentively

If the deli employee had communicated more effectively and acted like he was paying attention, Steve would have had more confidence that his order would be correct. Although he was in a hurry to get back to his office, he felt he needed to take the time to check his order before leaving the deli.

STEP 1
SAY WHAT YOU MEAN AND MEAN WHAT YOU SAY

When you communicate, you can either speak or listen. It is impossible to do both well at the same time. Communicating is a two-way exchange of information. Think of it as tossing a ball back and forth. The person who has the ball controls the conversation. As the speaker, you have the listener's attention, as long as you are sending a message that is meaningful and relevant to the conversation. When you have the ball, your main responsibility is to get your message across in a manner that the other person can interpret correctly. You accomplish that by thinking before speaking, choosing proper words, checking for understanding, and adding positive words to your message.

Think Before You Speak

When the ball gets tossed to you, take a moment to formulate your response. If the customer's request will require more time than you can quickly think of a good response, offer an interim one: "I'm going to have to do a little research before I can answer that. May I call you back today before 5 p.m. with the answer?" Now you can take time to think how you will respond.

Thinking on your feet is an important quality to develop. That means you need to have in your vocabulary some standard replies, such as communicating that you are happy to help and other basic courtesy phrases you may use to reply to customers' requests. Customers are usually okay if you do not have the answer immediately, as long as you offer to find the answer. They are *never* okay when you make up an answer.

Choose the Right Words and Speak Clearly

Choose words that will be understandable to the listener. State exactly what you mean in clear and precise terms. Speak assertively and confidently. Be specific and focus on communicating one thought at a time. Look at the customer when speaking. Give the customer a chance to respond. When you speak to a customer who may not be familiar with your company or products, choose words that will help convey the correct message. Opt for easy and familiar words. Trying to impress people with big words may only add confusion to your message.

Make Sure Your Tone Fits the Message You Are Sending

How you say something can be more important than what you say. When you did the verbal exercise on page 43 and asked a question four different ways, you got four different interpretations. In addition to choosing the right words, think about how you want to say them. When you talk to someone and use the wrong tone, your message may be misinterpreted. When speaking to a customer who is upset, use a serious, helpful tone. When offering assistance, use an enthusiastic tone. When asking a question, use a tone that shows you are truly interested in the answer. Pay attention to your listener's nonverbal cues—such as anger, confusion, or excitement—to make sure your tone fits your customer's emotions.

Add Welcoming Words to Your Vocabulary

You can enhance your message with welcoming words because they uplift, energize, and even encourage interest and excitement in your customers. When you use words that sound positive and confident, you will project a positive and confident attitude. Words and phrases like "Yes!," "I'll be happy to!," and "Sure I can!" send a message to your customers that you really are happy to help them. Words like "definitely" and "absolutely" send a message that you are enthusiastic and interested. Interjecting these and other welcoming words into your conversation conveys a sense of conviction that you truly want to help.

Keep Business Conversations Professional

When you interact with customers, draw the line between being professional and getting personal. Even though you may establish a friendly rapport, your customer is still your customer. Keep these conversations on a professional level.

TIP

When you are speaking with a customer for whom English is not the first language and the customer does not understand what you are saying, speak in the same tone and voice level but rephrase with different words—fewer if possible—to convey your message. It may help to break the message into short sentences. Stop after each sentence to gauge the customer's understanding. Simply repeating the same words over and over will most likely frustrate the customer—and you.

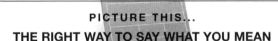

PICTURE THIS...
THE RIGHT WAY TO SAY WHAT YOU MEAN

Steve stopped at the local deli for lunch. He was in a hurry to place the order for himself and his coworkers and was greeted by an employee who looked at him, smiled, and enthusiastically said "Hi. Welcome to Max's Deli. How are you doing?"

"I'm doing great, thanks, but I am in a hurry. Is it possible to get my order quickly?"

"Yes, absolutely. I'll put a rush on it. What can I get for you?"

How Did the Customer Feel?

This time, the employee chose words that were appropriate, and he conveyed enthusiasm in his tone. Steve felt comfortable with the employee, and when the employee added "absolutely," Steve felt confident that he meant what he had said.

STEP 2
ENHANCE YOUR MESSAGES WITH NONVERBAL TECHNIQUES

The nonverbal signals you communicate may enhance or detract from the message you are sending. Nonverbal signals are even more important than the spoken word, because feelings and emotions are reflected outward and picked up through body language, expressions, gestures, and tone. Actions really do speak louder than words. No matter the reason you are communicating with customers, whether it is to sell a product or solve a problem, projecting interest and attention sends a positive message that you care about doing your best for your customers.

Body Language Communicates Volumes

Maintain a relaxed, open demeanor. Maintaining good posture sends the message that you are confident. When standing, hold your head high, stand straight, and allow your arms to fall naturally at your sides with your hands relaxed and open. When seated, maintain good posture by sitting up straight. If you need to cross your legs, do so at the ankles and fold your hands in your lap if seated away from your desk.

TIP

> Try this posture exercise: Pretend you have a string attached to the top of your head. Imagine the string is being pulled straight up until you are standing tall and holding your head in a comfortable position. When you find yourself slumping, do the string exercise.

Facial Expressions Communicate Volumes

Your face can be a snapshot of your feelings, so pay close attention and use your expressions to complete the message you are sending. Show enthusiasm, passion, concern, understanding, sincerity, believability, or other emotions to match your spoken message. Keep a pleasant facial expression when in a neutral situation by training your mouth muscles to turn slightly upward at the edges when you are in a relaxed pose. Nodding occasionally also conveys that you are attentive when listening.

A smile is one of the most powerful messages you can send. A smile translates into any language, to any age group, across any culture. Smile, and people will smile back at you. Try it. It does work. Get in the habit of smiling often. When you make it a habit to smile, your smile will look natural, not forced. A forced smile looks phony; sometimes a forced smile looks frozen on your face. When you smile often, your smile will become a natural part of your demeanor.

Eyes Communicate Volumes

Eye contact is one of the most important components of communication, yet it can be a tough habit to form. Wandering eyes send a message that you are bored or more interested in someone or something other than the person you are with. Making eye contact is a powerful tool. Eye contact shows you are interested, honest, and confident. When speaking, make a conscious effort to look at your customer and maintain a level of eye contact that is comfortable for both of you. Glance away occasionally and then bring your focus back so that you do not appear to be glaring. Be mindful of customers who appear uncomfortable with too much eye contact; in these situations, glance away more frequently.

Gestures Communicate Volumes

Gestures are also an effective nonverbal technique. They are used to emphasize a point, engage the listener, or express emotion. If you are in the habit of continually using your arms or hands to "help" you speak, try to refrain from doing so with customers. Rather, use gestures only occasionally. When gesturing, allow your motions to flow naturally. If they are too exaggerated, your customer will focus more on your movements than on your message. Also, never assume customers want to be touched. Always keep your hands to yourself.

Voice Tone Communicates Volumes

Voice tone is being re-addressed in this nonverbal technique section because your tone reflects outward what you are feeling inside. When you are feeling a particular emotion, you may unconsciously use an improper tone. Tone can improve on or detract from the message you are conveying. No matter what you are feeling inside, match the correct voice tone to the message you are speaking to your customer.

Some people have formed the habit of using upspeak in their voice tone, which is the tendency to end every sentence by raising voice pitch and sounding as though they are asking a question. Constantly speaking in this manner may sound annoying to your listener; so if you do this, break the habit.

Energy Level Communicates Volumes

Maintaining consistent energy may be difficult, especially if you work long hours. It is tough to operate effectively when you are tired, so try your best to get enough rest. When you are well rested, you will think clearly and stay attentive. Choosing healthful foods and snacks throughout your workday can help you sustain your energy level. Breathing deeply and doing a few stretches can help you sustain your energy level, and these can be done inconspicuously at your workstation.

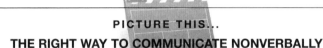

PICTURE THIS...
THE RIGHT WAY TO COMMUNICATE NONVERBALLY

Steve began to give his order: "I'll have a turkey and Swiss on whole wheat with mayo and tomatoes. . . ." As he spoke, he noticed that the employee looked directly at him before writing down the item. He smiled often, his posture told Steve he was interested, and he nodded occasionally as Steve spoke.

How Did the Customer Feel?

This time, the employee sent a message to Steve that he was interested in him as a customer. Steve felt relaxed as he waited for his order.

STEP 3
PUTTING WORDS TOGETHER: GRAMMAR USAGE

Proper grammar enhances the message being sent because it increases the chance that your customers will correctly understand what you are trying to convey. Casual grammar and shortcut vocabulary has become the norm and is acceptable to use when among friends, but not in a business setting. Using proper grammar helps set a professional tone and convey competence that will impress your customers.

Some common grammatical mistakes people make (and customers notice) are:

Putting yourself first when speaking of multiple people—

Incorrect: "Me and Jake will be taking care of you."

Correct: "Jake and I will be taking care of you."

Disagreement in number between nouns and verbs—

Incorrect: "He don't know what caused the problem."

Correct: "He doesn't know what caused the problem."

Using *ain't* and similar words—

Incorrect: "She ain't gonna do that."

Correct: "She isn't going to do that."

Use of double negatives—

Incorrect: "We would never do nothing like that."

Correct: "We would never do anything like that."

If you feel a need to brush up on your grammar skills, pick up a book on the subject and try to incorporate one new grammar rule at a time until you are comfortable.

Reflect Your Company's Personality

At work, you are the voice of your business, and you should always choose words that reflect your company's personality. In a deli setting, that personality will be fairly casual. In a fine dining restaurant, it will be more formal. If you are unclear how you should speak to customers, how friendly or casual you should be, ask your manager for guidance.

Speak Correctly

Using overly casual terms or running words together can be difficult for some people to understand. You already learned to say "yes" rather than "yeah." Get in the habit of always sounding out words in their correct form. Say "Hello" or "Hi" in place of "Hey, man." Say "What would you like to order?" or "What can I get you?" in place of "Whaddyawant?" Speak clearly, and you will present yourself as an intelligent, competent person.

Use Everyday Language

In Step 1, you learned that choosing the right words helps you send the right message to your listener. When you have a choice between two words, always opt for the simpler of the two. Keep your words short and simple whenever you can. They are easy for everyone to understand, and you do not risk the chance of sending the wrong message.

Avoid Using Technical Language, Shortcut Words, or Company Lingo

Your customers are not likely to know company terms, jargon, or acronyms, so stick to common, generic words. When you need to give technical explanations, convert difficult-to-understand words into words your customer will relate to. Always speak the language that your customers will understand. Try to match your speech to each customer's level of comprehension.

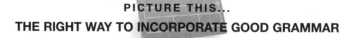

PICTURE THIS...
THE RIGHT WAY TO INCORPORATE GOOD GRAMMAR

The employee greeted Steve by saying "Hi. Welcome to Max's Deli. How are you doing?"

When it was time to take the order, he responded to Steve's statement about being in a hurry with "Yes, absolutely. I'll put a rush on it. What can I get for you?"

How Did the Customer Feel?

Steve appreciated that the employee used good grammar and was clear in his speech.

STEP 4

ASK THE CORRECT QUESTIONS AND ANSWER THE QUESTIONS CORRECTLY

Most of your customer interactions are going to involve asking and answering questions in order to satisfy their requests. Asking good questions is important in handling customers' requests correctly. Learning to ask focused questions will improve your communication skills, because that will help you gain a better understanding of what is necessary to satisfy your customers. Keeping your questions simple will help your customers process what information you need.

There Are Two Types of Questions: Open and Closed

Open questions require more than a yes-or-no answer: They are used to encourage the responder to provide information. Closed questions require only a one-word or short answer and are often used for clarification. In addition to asking questions, it is imperative to be able to respond appropriately when answering questions.

Keep Your Questions Simple

Stick to one question at a time. When you lump more than one question together, you run the risk that your customers may not register all the responses they need to give. If a question is long and involved or requires more than one answer, break it down. When you need to ask a series of questions, try interjecting some of the following statements in place of questions, so you will not sound as though you are interrogating your customer with a barrage of questions.

"Tell me about. . . ."

"Tell me more."

"I'd like to get more information on. . . ."

"Describe. . . ."

Ask Open Questions When You Need Information

Questions that require more than a one-word or short answer will get the customer talking. Open questions usually begin with *who, what, when, where, why,* and *how.* These types of questions are effective when you need more information to process a customer's request. Use open questions when you begin the questioning process to encourage your customer to talk, or when you need more information to handle a request.

"Who will be…?"

"What do you think about…?"

"What are…?"

"What type…?"

"When will…?"

"Where do you…?"

"Why is that…?"

"How do you…?"

"How will…?"

When you are finished asking questions and feel you have enough information to complete the request, summarize your understanding.

Be careful when asking a "why" question. For example, "Why do you want to do that?" may put your customer on the defensive. She might reply "It's none of your business." Smiling and using a reflective or helpful tone indicates you are asking out of interest to learn more about your customer's needs.

Ask Closed Questions to Control the Conversation

When you need short answers to clarify information or when you need a specific yes or no, choose closed questions. Questions beginning with "is," "are," "do," "can," or "will" require only a yes or no answer. Questions beginning with "who," "would," "how," or "where" require a short answer. Closed questions are good to use toward the end of the questioning portion of your contact to narrow down the information you need so you can help your customer. Closed questions are also effective in guiding your customer to make a decision.

"Is ___ enough…?"

"Are you…?"

"Do you think…?"

"Will you…?"

"Who will…?"

"Would you like…?"

"How many…?"

"Where do you…?"

Winding down your questioning period with closed questions will help you interpret and confirm the customer's request and will also guide your customer to finalize a decision. "Does that sound good to you?" If the customer is undecided or sounds confused, circle back to an open question: "What questions do you have?"

Before Answering a Customer's Question,
Check for Understanding

If you do not clearly understand the question, recap it or ask a clarifying question rather than guessing an answer. It is better to ask another question than to answer the wrong question. Also, never answer a question unless you are sure your answer is accurate. It is better to say "I don't know" than to give an answer that may be incorrect. If you do not know, say so; follow up with "I'll find out for you." Remember to always focus on what you *can* do, rather than on what you *can't*. If a customer asks you to do something you cannot do, say "Here's what I can do for you. . . ."

TIP

When a customer asks for another employee who is not available, never say that the employee is at lunch, on break, went home early, has not come in yet, or that you do not know where the employee is. Rather, say "_____ is unavailable now. How may I help you?" or "_____ is out of the office now. I'll be happy to help you."

Always Try to Give More
Than Just a One-Word Answer

No matter which questioning technique customers use, try to answer as though the customer is asking an open question. Try to give customers sufficient information to help them make decisions. Giving more than a one-word answer can have an added bonus: You can generate sales. For example, if a customer asks, "I saw this in blue at a friend's home. Can you order it in blue?" you may answer, "Yes." Or . . . "Yes, I can. I can also order it in hunter green, cranberry, and gold. It's really pretty in those colors and looks great paired." Now the customer has options from which to choose. She may decide to order more than one, helping to increase the employee's sales.

BRAINSTORM

As a group, discuss the reasons you might need to ask questions of your customers. Together, come up with typical open and closed questions you should ask to best serve their needs.

Answering questions with more than one-word answers can be difficult at times. Think about some closed questions your customers might ask you and come up with answers that are more than "yes" or "no."

PICTURE THIS...
THE RIGHT WAY TO ASK QUESTIONS

Steve finished his order: ". . . a ham on rye with mustard and a pastrami on rye with mustard."

"What else would you like?"

"Do you have potato salad?"

"We sure do. We also have cole slaw, baked beans, and pasta salad."

"Hmm, I'll take a small order of potato salad."

"Would you like any other sides?"

"No, thanks."

"Okay. Just one more thing. Do you want spicy or regular mustard on the sandwiches?"

"Regular."

How Did the Customer Feel?

Because the employee asked a combination of open and closed questions, Steve felt confident that the order had been written down correctly. He also appreciated the employee asking him if he wanted anything else.

STEP 5
OVERCOME THE BIG NO

You will absolutely, definitely, positively work with customers who end up saying no. No matter how well you ask and answer questions, and no matter how on-target your proposed solution, you will deal with customers who object to your proposals. When you offer a valid solution and your customer says no, your job is to uncover the reasons for the objection. If you work in sales, it may also be your job to find ways to persuade the customer to say yes. The bottom line, always, is to do what is right for the customer. Never offer or try to sell a customer something he or she does not need just to make a sale. Being able to get to the real reason for the objection will enable you to figure out the best solution for that particular customer.

Listen to the Customer's Objection

When a customer says no, an objection has been made to your proposed solution. To learn the reason behind the no, ask a combination of open and closed questions. You need to understand why the customer is saying no so you can best help him or her. For example, you just made a sales proposal for a complete home-security system, and the customer says no. You might ask: "You seem hesitant. What type of security are you interested in for your home?" The customer's responses might be: "Something a little cheaper" or "This one seems too complicated."

Acknowledge the Objection

Always validate the customer's reason, and then respond with a positive statement. For example, if you gather that the objection was due to cost, you might say "I understand the price seems high, but our system offers full security in case of fire and break-in. When you consider that, it isn't as expensive as it seems." Or "At first it may seem complicated, but once you learn how to use it, it becomes second nature." Doing this shows that you empathize with the customer's objection. Adding specific benefits reinforces the solution you proposed.

Follow Up with a Question

The customer objected. You listened to the objection, acknowledged it, asked questions to uncover the reason for the objection, and gave more information about your proposal. Next, you need to follow up. By following up with a clarifying question, you will know how to proceed. "How does that sound?" or "What do you think about that?"

Consider the Customer's Answer

The customer's response will determine whether she is objecting because she does not agree with your proposal, or whether she is looking for more information. If the customer responds with something like "How much did you say it will cost?" she is interested in more information about the product. However, if she answers "I really can't afford that," proceed with caution. If you have other products to offer, you can ask "What were you looking to spend?" The customer's response will help you determine whether to continue. If, after proposing an alternate solution, the customer still says no, validate the customer's decision. "I understand, and I'm sorry I wasn't able to help you."

TIP

Always be truthful when stating your point of view or the benefits of a product. Never try to make a sale or glorify the point you are attempting to make to get the customer to agree with you. When you are not truthful, you will come across in an insincere manner and the customer will figure out what you are doing.

PICTURE THIS...
THE RIGHT WAY TO HANDLE OBJECTIONS

"Would you like any other sides?" the deli employee asked.

"No one asked for anything," Steve responded.

"We do have a large-size potato salad which is great for sharing."

"Hmm, I'm not sure."

"The larger size only costs two dollars more than the price for the small size. How does that sound?"

"Okay, that sounds good."

"Great. Just one more thing: Do you want spicy or regular mustard?"

"Regular."

How Did the Customer Feel?

Steve liked the fact that even though he said no, the employee gave him another option, and then asked a follow-up question. If the employee had not asked, Steve would not have thought about ordering the larger size, and he was glad he had because his coworkers shared it.

STEP 6
LISTEN ATTENTIVELY

In Step 1, you learned that it is impossible to speak and listen at the same time and do both well. Speaking is important because you are delivering a message, but listening is even more important than speaking. Without the ability to listen well, communication can never be effective. If you do not listen to the message, you might: misinterpret or assume you understand; give the wrong response; or need to ask the customer to repeat. When any of these things occur, you will not make a good impression on your customer.

Be Aware of Barriers to Listening

Barriers to listening are the distractions that make it difficult to focus and pay attention. Barriers may be caused by external circumstances, such as a noisy workplace, a loud coworker, people walking by, or someone talking to you when you are trying to listen to your customer. You may also unwittingly cause internal barriers to listening by trying to pay attention to two people at the same time, multitasking, thinking of your response while the customer is still speaking, assuming you know what the customer wants, or interrupting and finishing someone's thought. Emotional listening also creates a barrier to listening. When you get caught up in and mirror someone else's emotions, it is difficult to stay objective.

Distractions are going to occur. Sometimes it is going to be difficult to listen. Understanding your personal barriers will help you shut them out so that you can focus and listen completely.

Focus Entirely on Your Customer

Think of the customer you are helping as the only customer in your business. When you do this, you will be able to give him or her your full attention. Shut out distractions. When you are listening to the customer, stay interested, even if your customer's message is long. When that happens, you can show empathy in your facial expressions or by nodding to indicate that you are following what the customer is saying. When you nod occasionally and say something like "I see," "tell me more," or even "hmm," you show you are still listening. If your customer rambles or gets off track, wait for a pause, politely interrupt, and ask some clarifying questions to take control of the conversation.

Listen Completely

When you try to listen and talk at the same time, you do not do either effectively. Pay attention to the speaker. You are going to get the ball tossed back to you and when it is your turn to speak you will want the other person to pay attention. Try not to think of your response when the speaker is still talking. Wait until the message is winding down before thinking about how you want to respond. Unless you hear the customer's complete statement or question, you might come up with an incorrect response.

Handle Interruptions Professionally

If someone else interrupts you, and it is an avoidable interruption, explain to the interrupter that you will be with him as soon as you are done helping your customer. If it is an unavoidable interruption, excuse yourself momentarily from your customer to answer the other person. Then quickly return your attention and apologize for the interruption.

Remain Objective; Do Not Judge

Before drawing a conclusion or making a judgment, gather as much information as you can. This will help you avoid jumping to conclusions. If you are not sure you understand correctly, paraphrase the customer's words or ask more questions to gather additional information.

Employ Nonverbal Listening Strategies

You learned about nonverbal communication and how important it is to pay attention to your mannerisms when speaking. Paying attention to your customers' nonverbal signals will increase your ability to listen attentively. A person may say one thing but convey a completely different message through nonverbal signals, so pay attention to your customer's body language and facial expressions to help you respond appropriately. If a customer appears upset, on edge, or angry, convey empathy in your response.

You also demonstrate that you are listening attentively by the nonverbal signals you send. When you are face to face, turn toward your customer. Maintain eye contact. Nod from time to time to show you are paying attention to a long message. Match your facial expressions to the message. If you are unsure, maintain a neutral facial expression. When speaking by phone, you can interject an occasional comment to show you are paying attention, such as "I understand" or "Oh, my!"

Check for Understanding

The last part of listening attentively is to make sure you interpreted the message correctly. Doing so will clear up misunderstandings and sends the message that you were listening, and it can also show that you understand the customer's point of view. Take a moment to recap, question, and summarize what you have heard. Then you will confidently be able to find the best resolution for each customer.

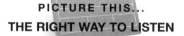

PICTURE THIS...
THE RIGHT WAY TO LISTEN

"Okay, you mentioned you were in a hurry, so I'll put a rush on your order," the deli employee told Steve. "It should be out very soon."

Throughout their interaction, the employee made eye contact as he wrote down Steve's order. He also asked questions to clarify the order. And, since he could tell Steve was in a hurry, he responded accordingly.

How Did the Customer Feel?

Because Steve felt he received great customer service, he thought *I'm going to come here more often for lunch.*

PICTURE THIS...
PUTTING IT ALL TOGETHER

Steve stopped at the local deli for lunch. He was in a hurry to place the order for himself and his coworkers, and he was greeted by an employee who looked at him, smiled, and enthusiastically said "Hi. Welcome to Max's Deli. How are you doing?"

"I'm doing great, thanks, but I am in a hurry. Is it possible to get my order quickly?"

"Yes, absolutely. I'll put a rush on it. What can I get you?"

Steve began to give his order. "I'll have a turkey and Swiss on whole wheat with mayo and tomatoes. . . ." As he spoke, he noticed that the employee looked directly at him before writing down the item. He smiled often, his posture told Steve he was interested, and he nodded occasionally as Steve spoke.

Steve finished his order. ". . . a ham on rye with mustard and a pastrami on rye with mustard."

"What else would you like?"

"Do you have potato salad?"

"We sure do. We also have cole slaw, baked beans, and pasta salad."

"I'll take a side order of potato salad."

"Would you like any other sides?" the deli employee asked.

"No one asked for anything," Steve responded.

"We do have a larger-size potato salad which is great for sharing."

"Hmm, I'm not sure."

"The larger size only costs two dollars more than the price for the small size. How does that sound?"

"Okay, that sounds good."

"Great. Just one more thing. Do you want spicy or regular mustard?"

"Regular."

"Okay. You mentioned you were in a hurry, so I'll put a rush on your order," the deli employee told Steve. "It should be out very soon."

No matter where you work, you can apply the principles of communicating effectively to your interactions with your customers. Think before you speak, be aware of your nonverbal messages, use good grammar, ask the correct questions and answer questions correctly, handle objections effectively—and above all, listen, listen, listen.

BUSINESS NØT AS USUAL

Effective Communication Is the Firm Foundation upon Which You Build Strong Relationships

It's happened to all of us. Someone you thought you knew—perhaps a friend or a family member—did something dishonest or disrespectful to you, causing you to lose trust in that person. When trust is lost, it takes a long time to regain it. The same goes for business dealings. Unlike personal relationships, where working to rebuild trust is vital to maintain the relationship, customers will not give you a second chance if they feel they have been lied to or disrespected. Can you afford to lose your customers? Think about it: In any business environment, holding on to your existing customers is much easier than trying to find new ones. When you communicate truthfully and respectfully, you send a powerful message—you show your customers that you value and appreciate them, and they are far more likely to value and appreciate you.

- Actions always speak louder than words.

- Honesty is always the best policy.

- To your customers, *you* are the company.

- Represent your company well by communicating effectively.

- Never do anything to cause a customer to lose trust in you.

K E Y   P O I N T S

Step 1: Say What You Mean and Mean What You Say

- Think before you speak.

- Choose the right words and speak clearly.

- Make sure your tone fits the message you are sending.

- Add welcoming words to your vocabulary.

- Keep business conversations professional.

Step 2: Enhance Your Messages with Nonverbal Techniques

- Body language communicates volumes.

- Facial expressions communicate volumes.

- Eyes communicate volumes.

- Gestures communicate volumes.

- Voice tone communicates volumes.

- Energy level communicates volumes.

Step 3: Putting Words Together: Grammar Usage

- Reflect your company's personality.

- Speak correctly.

- Use everyday language.

- Avoid using technical language, shortcut words, or company lingo.

Step 4: Ask the Correct Questions and Answer the Questions Correctly

- Keep your questions simple.

- Ask open questions when you need information.

- Ask closed questions to control the conversation.

- Before answering a customer's question, check for understanding.

- Always try to give more than a one-word answer.

Step 5: Overcome the Big No

- Listen to the customer's objection.
- Acknowledge the objection.
- Follow up with a question.
- Consider the customer's answer.

Step 6: Listen Attentively

- Be aware of barriers to listening.
- Focus entirely on your customer.
- Listen completely.
- Handle interruptions professionally.
- Remain objective; do not judge.
- Employ nonverbal listening strategies.
- Check for understanding.

PRACTICE LESSON

Step 1: Say What You Mean and Mean What You Say

Make a list of words and phrases you will incorporate into your vocabulary.

_____

_____

Step 2: Enhance Your Messages with Nonverbal Techniques

Write examples of what you will do to improve your nonverbal communication.

_____

_____

Step 3: Putting Words Together: Grammar Usage

Think about your grammar and list some things you can do to improve it.

_____

_____

Step 4: Ask the Correct Questions and Answer the Questions Correctly

Think about your typical customer contacts and write examples of open and closed questions you will use.

_____

_____

Step 5: Overcome the Big No

Think about a recent customer contact in which the customer objected. Using the questioning techniques, write how you would handle the customer.

_____

_____

Step 6: Listen Attentively

Write examples of how you can improve your listening skills.

_____

_____

D O I N G   I T   R I G H T !

Whenever I need a print job done, Donna is my go-to person. The first time we met, I had an unusual job to complete. As I explained what I wanted, Donna looked directly at me, listened well, and paid attention while I showed her the document. She asked me some questions to make sure she understood correctly, and she took notes as I answered. She assured me that she would take care of my job. I knew I was in good hands.

Later that day, Donna called me. "I started printing out your job, but the pages look odd to me. Before I continue, I just want to double check that I have this right. . . ." I answered her questions, assured her that she did have it right, and thanked her for calling to check.

When I drove to pick up my order the next day, I was confident that it had been done correctly. I wasn't disappointed. "I really appreciate that you took the time to call yesterday," I complimented Donna. "That meant a lot to me."

"It just looked so weird," she said with a smile. "I didn't want you to drive all the way here only to find out it wasn't what you wanted." That was the exact moment that I knew I could rely on Donna. For someone to care that much told me that she truly valued me as a customer.

Other companies might be less expensive. They might even have a faster turnaround time. That doesn't really matter to me. When you find someone good, you stay with her.

H O W   D O   I   M E A S U R E   U P ?

1. When I communicate with my customers, do I remember to think before I speak so I choose the right words? What internal cues can I use in order to always present myself professionally?

_____

_____

2. What nonverbal messages am I sending? What am I good at? What can I do to improve?

    _____

    _____

3. How is my grammar? What are my bad habit "words" and what can I do to stop using them?

    _____

    _____

4. Do I ask a combination of open and closed questions to make sure I understand my customers' requests? In the typical situations where I stumble, what can I do to correct myself?

    _____

    _____

5. What are my external and internal barriers that make listening difficult?

    _____

    _____

Jumping In with Both Feet: Relationship Building

**RELATIONSHIP BUILDING IS THE
CORNERSTONE OF CUSTOMER SERVICE**

Establishing strong relationships builds on the principles you have learned so far: making a great first impression, speaking and acting courteously and respectfully, communicating effectively, and listening attentively. While this may seem difficult if you do not handle repeat customers, even when customers do business with a company only once, they remember and judge the company based on their interaction with its employees. They remember whether their interaction was good or bad, and they are likely to share their experiences with others. As a result, your customers can be your best—or your worst—marketing and advertising tools.

CUSTOMER SERVICE IS
BUILDING RELATIONSHIPS

From the moment customers form their first impressions to the moment you complete your interactions, you have a valuable opportunity to build relationships. The same applies to those customers who may visit only once or sporadically. When you interact positively and go out of your way to help each customer, you build a relationship. And when those customers receive great service, they will remember and will tell others about their positive experiences.

When you are courteous and have a positive attitude toward your customers, you show that you care. When you demonstrate good communication skills by thinking before you speak, keeping your nonverbal body language relaxed and open, and using correct grammar, you present yourself as knowledgeable and confident. When you ask the correct questions to help the customer and answer questions the customer asks you, you present yourself as a competent employee. When listening attentively, you demonstrate that you are truly interested in each and every customer.

You are off to a good start in learning how to provide great customer service. The next step is learning how to build relationships. You interact with customers in two ways: You work to build new relationships, and you work to maintain ongoing relationships. Without new business relationships, your company will not grow. Without ongoing business relationships, you will not develop the loyal customer base that sustains your business.

Building and maintaining positive relationships is based on the principles of basic courtesies and effective communication. Your relationship begins when a customer forms a favorable impression of you. It continues when you establish rapport. You can do this by asking a question as simple as "How are you today?" and then listening and responding appropriately to the customer's answer. From these first few words with a customer, you have the opportunity to respond in a positive, upbeat manner. For example, if the customer says that she is not doing well, you may respond "I'm sorry to hear that. What can I do to help you?" Showing interest helps to establish rapport.

You can take advantage of those first few minutes with a customer to find common ground. Finding common ground means discovering an interest you share. It can also mean being able to relate to the other person. That may be as simple as responding to a customer's comment about the weather. If the customer says "It's so cold outside I wish I was in Florida," you might respond "I can't agree more. In fact, my husband and I are thinking of planning a vacation there."

When you establish rapport and find common ground, your next step is showing that you are helpful and interested in finding the right solution for your customers. Asking and answering questions to identify what the customer needs, and then doing all you can to take care of the request will make each customer feel valued.

When customers do repeat business with your company, you have the opportunity to maintain an ongoing relationship by remembering them and by learning their tastes and preferences. As for the customer who was not having a good day, the next time you communicate with her, you might say "Hi, Mrs. Adams, I hope you're having a better day today." Think how special Mrs. Adams will feel, knowing that she was important enough to you to remember something about her.

In business, you will deal with many different types of customers. Hopefully, most will be pleasant and easy to satisfy. Some personality types, however, will present challenges that can fluster you. And some may have disabilities that make you feel uncomfortable if you do not know the appropriate words to say or actions to take. Learning how to interact positively with various personalities and disabilities will enable you to confidently handle any customer in any situation. You will be on your way to establishing and maintaining high-quality relationships with all your customers.

BRAINSTORM

Before we jump in with both feet and learn how to build and maintain positive relationships, let's take a step back and identify the answers to three important questions that will help you to understand how best to form relationships with your customers:

- Who are your customers?

- What do they expect from your business?

- How do your products and services enhance their lives?

Discuss and answer these questions. Then you will have a better idea of how to establish rapport with your customers because you already have general information about them. This will give you what you need to find common ground and begin building relationships.

PICTURE THIS...
THE WRONG WAY TO BUILD RELATIONSHIPS

Sarah was an unlikely customer service employee. She was home from college for summer break and took a part-time job at a women's clothing shop in the local mall. Sarah had not worked in retail before, and she was unsure about how to interact with customers. Her job was to greet customers and help them find what they needed. On her first day, her manager explained her job duties, showed her where to locate stock in the back room, and told her to be friendly to customers.

"Be sure you say hello to the customers when they come in," her manager said as she walked away.

Sarah busied herself folding tops on the front display table.

Beth Adams, meanwhile, was outside the store looking at the clothing display in the window. She came into the store and noticed Sarah.

This was Sarah's first customer. She nervously said "Hi," barely speaking above a whisper as she quickly glanced at the woman and then back down to her work. Sarah continued to fold the tops while the woman browsed.

"Excuse me. Can you see if you have this skirt in a size twelve?" Beth asked.

Sarah nodded, took the item from Beth, and retreated into the stock room without saying a word or making eye contact. When Sarah came back, she said "Sorry, we don't have it." She spoke softly and looked at the floor as she spoke.

"Oh, all right. Well, thanks for checking." Beth walked out of the store.

What Went Wrong?

Even though Sarah knew she would have to deal with customers, she did not understand the importance of building relationships. She wanted to work in this clothing store to get the employee discount, and had not thought about her duties or the customers.

Sarah's manager had incorrectly assumed that Sarah knew how to interact well with customers; but if they had discussed the answers to the three questions above, Sarah would have had a better idea of who their customers were and what they expected.

In this situation, Sarah's manager should have discussed customers' expectations and ensured that Sarah knew how to interact with them. She should also have explained whether the job duties involved helping customers select outfits, or whether they should be allowed to browse without assistance. In addition, it would have been helpful to Sarah if she had known whether she would interact with the same customers regularly and if she should introduce herself and get to know their individual tastes and styles.

If the manager had discussed how the store's products enhanced its customers' lives, Sarah would have known how to help the customers more effectively. If this was an expensive boutique where the customers were interested in designer labels, Sarah could show customers where to find specific items. If the store stocked trendy clothes, Sarah could show customers the latest fashions and hot items.

The responsibility for what went wrong in this scenario lies with both the manager and Sarah. Although her manager showed Sarah where to locate stock in the back room and how to keep the displays neat, and told her to be friendly to the customers, she did not make sure that Sarah understood. Likewise, Sarah did not ask questions to make sure she understood her job responsibilities. From a manager's perspective, it is never a good idea to assume employees know how to interact with customers. From an employee's perspective, it is always a good idea to ask questions and learn about the customers with whom you will interact.

How Did the Customer Feel?

Sarah did not make a good first impression. She should have made eye contact, smiled, and greeted Beth in a friendly, helpful manner. When Beth asked for a specific skirt, she got the impression that Sarah was not interested in helping her. To change that, Sarah could have said "I'll be happy to check on that," or "Absolutely. I'll be glad to see if we have that." Because Sarah acted disinterested, Beth did not feel valued, and she was ambivalent about shopping in that store.

By learning the six steps below, you will learn how to build and maintain positive and strong relationships with all your customers.

Step 1: Establish Rapport

Step 2: Interact Positively with Customers

Step 3: Identify Customers' Needs

Step 4: Make Each Customer Feel Valued

Step 5: Maintain Ongoing Relationships

Step 6: Understand Various Types of Customers

Doing a good job and building strong relationships is a two-way street. Both the manager and the employee need to be clear on customer expectations. Asking and answering questions will uncover any inconsistencies. Even in a store where customers may visit only occasionally, employees can work on developing relationships with them. Every customer interaction, even short-term ones, results in a relationship.

STEP 1
ESTABLISH RAPPORT

Establishing rapport begins the moment you start communicating with your customers. Smiling at a customer can help establish rapport by showing you are interested. Being friendly is a great way to establish rapport because you demonstrate that you are approachable and willing to help, and that can put customers at ease. Staying interested and picking up on cues from your customers will help you establish rapport. For example, if a customer says "I'm having a terrible day," and you respond by saying "I'm sorry to hear that. I hope I can help improve your day," you demonstrate consideration toward your customer's feelings. Finding ground is another way to establish rapport because it shows you are able to relate to the other person. When the customer said she was having a bad day, responding with "I'm sorry to hear that. I had one of those days yesterday" shows empathy toward your customer's feelings. When you do these things customers will have faith that you will do all you can to take care of their needs.

Establishing rapport will depend on your customer interactions. Think about your place of employment and the answers you identified in the Brainstorm on page 74:

> *Who are my customers?* Are they men, women, tweens, teens, young adults, or all age groups?

> *What do they expect from my company?* Do they expect quality products? Good value? The best prices? Quick service? Products that enhance their self-image? A large selection? The latest styles?

> *How do my company's products and services enhance the customers' lives?* Do they make the customers' lives easier? Are they a necessity? Do they make our customers feel good about themselves?

When you know the answers to these questions, you will have a good idea how to relate to your customers. Armed with this knowledge, you can begin to establish rapport with them, which is the first step of relationship-building.

Be Friendly

No matter who your customers are, everyone appreciates someone who is friendly. When you smile and offer a friendly greeting, you show that you are a person who is approachable.

Be Interested

A smile and friendly greeting also show that you are interested. When you ask people how they are doing or how you can help, you convey the message that you are interested. Being interested means listening when customers speak. Imagine how you would sound if you asked a customer how he was doing and he said "I'm having the worst day of my life. Really awful," and with no emotion you responded "Oh"—or, worse, continued the conversation with no comment. The customer most likely would wonder why you had even bothered to ask. Being interested means listening and responding accordingly. Being interested means doing your best to help each customer.

Be Considerate

If a customer says he is upset by a previous contact with an employee, you might say "I'm sorry to hear that. What can I do to help you?" Not only are you showing consideration, you are showing that you are sensitive to the customer's situation. And even if you cannot personally understand or relate to what the customer is saying, you can always be considerate in your response by displaying empathy.

Find Common Ground

When you listen to your customer's statements and responses, try to find something that you have in common. To the customer who is upset about prior treatment by your company, you might respond "I'm sorry to hear that. I wouldn't like being treated like that. That should never happen." The customer will appreciate that you can relate to his experience. Even if you cannot relate to the customer's experience, there are other ways to find common ground. Empathize with the customer. Ask a question. Show interest. Compliment the customer. Say something about yourself. Or talk about the weather!

Be Trustful

The best way to demonstrate that you can be trusted is by being honest and ethical in everything you do. When you always act with integrity, your personality reflects your honesty. If you are friendly and helpful with a customer and later make fun of him within earshot of other customers, you do not come across as being a trustful person. Being trustful includes treating people with dignity and respect.

PICTURE THIS...
THE RIGHT WAY TO ESTABLISH RAPPORT

"Be sure you say hello to the customers when they come in," her manager said as she walked away.

Sarah stopped her and asked, "When I say hi to customers, am I supposed to ask if they need help, or should I leave them alone?"

"That's a good question. Most of our customers are working women who come in to browse, so we usually leave them alone. But do let them know you are here to help if they need anything." The manager noticed that Sarah seemed hesitant. "Here's an example. When a customer comes in, smile, make eye contact, and say something like 'Hi, how are you today? If you need anything, I'll be happy to help you.' That way, the customer knows we're going to allow her to browse without being pushy, but will be available to help."

"Oh, okay. Thanks." Sarah busied herself folding tops on the front display table.

Beth Adams, meanwhile, was outside the store looking at the clothing display in the window. She came into the store and noticed Sarah.

This was Sarah's first customer. She was nervous but knew what she needed to do. She looked at Beth, smiled, and said "Hi, how are you doing today?"

Beth smiled back. "I'm fine, thanks, how are you?"

"It's my first day, so I don't know yet. I'm a little nervous."

"I know how that feels. I'm sure you'll do just fine."

"If you need anything, I'll be happy to help you."

"Thanks. I'm looking for a skirt. I'll look around."

"Okay. We have skirts in great summer colors."

Beth smiled and walked away.

How Did the Customer Feel?

Even though Sarah felt awkward, she showed that she was approachable when she smiled and greeted Beth. Beth appreciated the interest Sarah displayed by listening and commenting on the skirts in great summer colors. When she told Beth it was her first day and she was nervous, Beth could relate to her feelings and they found common ground. Beth felt comfortable with Sarah, who had established rapport with her.

STEP 2
INTERACT POSITIVELY WITH CUSTOMERS

When you convey an interest in establishing rapport with your customers, continue building your relationships by interacting with them in a positive manner. When you are positive and upbeat, people will respond likewise. By trying to find ways to surprise them with good service, you show your customers you care about doing your best.

Be Helpful

Show your customers that you care. Go the extra mile for them. Explain to your customers what you are doing to respond to their requests. Try to give them a little more than they asked for. Do something to make other people feel good. When you set a personal goal to help someone every day, you will find ways to meet that goal, and it is a great habit to form. When you do something nice for someone, you will feel good.

Be a Problem Solver

Customers may look to you to solve a problem. Be part of the solution rather than part of the problem by seeking the best answers rather than focusing on what is wrong. When you adopt a problem-solving approach, you will find ways to make things right. People who focus on solutions find ways to make things better. Always tell customers what you *can* do, rather than what you cannot do.

Be Credible

This means being knowledgeable about your products and your company. It also means being honest. Customers appreciate nice employees, but they value knowledgeable employees who are truthful. Learn as much as you can about your product line. If you need additional technical training, ask your manager for it. Never lie to your customers or make false claims. When you pair knowledge with ethical behavior, you have a winning combination.

Believe in Your Products

Believing that your products will help your customers is crucial to doing the right thing for them. No matter what your company manufactures or sells, whether it is life insurance or clothing or deli sandwiches, you need to believe that your products add value to your customers' lives. When you truly believe that your company's products can help your customers, you will promote your products, your company, and yourself in a positive and sincere manner.

PICTURE THIS...
THE RIGHT WAY TO INTERACT POSITIVELY

Sarah continued to fold the tops while Beth browsed.

"Excuse me. Can you see if you have this skirt in a size twelve?" Beth asked.

Sarah took the skirt from Beth and said "Yes, I'll be happy to. I love this shade of green."

"I love it too. I hope you have it; I've been looking for a green skirt."

"I'll be right back." Sarah hurried into the stock room. She came back with a different style green skirt and said, "I'm sorry, we don't have that skirt in your size. I don't know if you saw this one. I brought it because you mentioned you wanted a green skirt."

"Thanks, but that isn't exactly what I was looking for."

How Did the Customer Feel?

Beth felt that Sarah was helpful. And because she demonstrated that she was solution-oriented by bringing a different green skirt, Beth had a positive feeling about her.

S T E P 3
IDENTIFY CUSTOMERS' NEEDS

Customers come into your business for a reason. Sometimes they are not very clear about their needs. Beth was specific when she mentioned she was looking for a green skirt. This helped Sarah come up with an alternate option. If Beth had not mentioned her preference for green, Sarah might have shown her the same style in red. While this is a simplistic example, the principle is the same in any business. When you deal with customers, your job is to uncover their needs, whether they offer what they are looking for or you need to discover it.

Ask Questions

In Chapter 2, you learned about open and closed questions. When customers do not know how to tell you what they need, it is your job to figure it out. Sometimes customers are not even sure they know what they need. Use open questions to get the customer talking. Remember, questions that begin with "what," "why," and "how" encourage customers to talk. Use closed questions to clarify an answer. Closed questions begin with "who," "would," "how," and "where." A question beginning with "how" can be either open or closed: Open: "How do you think you would use this?" Closed: "How many times a week will you use it?"

Summarize Customers' Needs

After you have asked enough questions to determine your customer's needs, summarize your understanding of what he or she has told you. For example, "From what I understand, your son has allergies, and you are looking for a vacuum cleaner that will remove the greatest number of allergens and is the least costly," or "You mentioned that you got your bill and you were overcharged for. . . ." If your understanding is incorrect, ask more questions until you feel you understand; then summarize again.

Recommend Appropriate Solutions

When you ask enough questions, you get enough information to recommend the best solution. If your job is to sell products, you can make an appropriate proposal. If you handle billing issues or technical support, you can find a workable solution. Make sure that your recommendations are based on what the customer told you. Refer to things the customer said when making your recommendation. "This is our most economic vacuum, and it will remove 99 percent of all allergens. With your son's allergies, you want to make sure your vacuum picks up as many allergen particles as possible." Always offer tailored solutions based on the customer's specific needs. Customers are not one-size-fits-all, and neither are solutions.

Handle Objections

As you learned in Chapter 2, customers are not always going to buy into your proposed solutions. When that happens, listen to the customer's objection. Acknowledge it. Follow up with a question. Or questions. Consider the customer's answer. Example: Following up on the vacuum cleaner sale, the customer says "Thanks, I'll think about it." You respond, "What questions do you have about this one?" "I don't have any questions, but it's more than I wanted to spend." You continue, "I can understand that, but this product is the most efficient for removing allergens. We do have less expensive models that I can show you."

TIP

Even when your customer does not ask, always answer the question "What is this going to do for me?" Whenever you propose a solution, your customer is silently answering this question. When you establish a relationship with a customer by asking enough questions to know specifically where your customer is coming from, it will be easier for you to help him or her find the right solution for their needs.

THE RIGHT WAY TO IDENTIFY CUSTOMERS' NEEDS

"Thanks, but that isn't exactly what I was looking for."

"What type of skirt are you interested in?"

"I prefer longer skirts."

"What other colors would you be interested in?"

"I really wanted green, but I suppose I could use a khaki skirt."

"Do you care for prints?"

"No, I only wear solids."

"I'll check to see if we have the style you liked in khaki. I'll also see if we have other longer skirts in a solid green or khaki. I'll be right back."

"Thank you. That would be great."

How Did the Customer Feel?

Beth was pleasantly surprised when Sarah asked questions to determine exactly what she was looking for, recapped what Beth said to make sure she understood, and made a recommendation to look for another style of skirt. Getting this level of caring service stood out in Beth's mind.

STEP 4
MAKE EACH CUSTOMER FEEL VALUED

When you establish rapport, interact positively, and identify customers' needs to make the best recommendation, you are on your way to building strong relationships. Your next step is to say something to show your customers that you value their business. Whether your interaction is a one-time conversation or an ongoing interaction with a customer who does repeat business with your company, your primary job is to communicate effectively and build positive relationships. Even in instances in which customers do not agree with your proposals or you do not have what they are looking for, you can still say something to show that you value them.

Go out of Your Way for Your Customers

Do all you can to help them and always try to do more than they expect. When a customer asks a question, give a thorough explanation rather than a one-word answer. Sarah could have easily let Beth walk out the door when she could not find the skirt she wanted. By going out of her way, she not only made Beth feel valued, she also had the possibility of making a sale.

Validate Customers' Decisions

If a customer agrees to your proposal, say something supportive. "That's a great choice. I know you'll be happy with it." In situations in which customers do not agree with your suggestions, say something to justify their decisions. If the vacuum salesperson did not make the sale, he could say "I understand how you feel. This brand is costly." Doing so would make the mother feel better about her decision.

Instill Positive Feelings

Always make customers feel good about their decisions. Think how the mother would feel if the salesperson ended the conversation by saying "I guess your son will have to deal with the allergens in your house." Rather, he might follow up with a positive statement: "It's a big decision. I'll be happy to help you if you have any more questions about it." Think how Beth would feel if Sarah replied "You want green? Green is such a drab color. Why not go for a bright color like pink?" Sarah instilled positive feelings by saying that Beth's choice was a great color. Always make sure your last words are memorable ones that instill positive feelings about yourself and your company.

PICTURE THIS...
THE RIGHT WAY TO MAKE CUSTOMERS FEEL VALUED

Sarah returned with a skirt. "I found this khaki skirt. How do you like it?"

After looking it over, Beth said "Thanks for looking, but I still like the style of the green one better."

"I understand and I appreciate that you really liked that skirt. I hope next time you come in, we have the styles and colors you like."

How Did the Customer Feel?

Sarah went out of her way to find another skirt, but when Beth said it was not what she was looking for, Sarah validated Beth's decision by saying she understood. She instilled positive feelings in Beth by assuring her that she appreciated her decision.

STEP 5
MAINTAIN ONGOING RELATIONSHIPS

When you build strong relationships with customers, your work is not done. In any relationship, you have to work to maintain strong bonds. Customers come back a second time because you have established a relationship with them. Imagine how valued they will feel if you remember them! Because Sarah went out of her way to help Beth, Beth is likely to return. That is the way to build customer loyalty.

Remember Your Customers

Nothing makes a customer feel more valued than being remembered. Acknowledge your repeat customers by saying something to show that you remember them. Customers who do repeat business with a company appreciate being recognized. As for the customer who was having his worst day, think how he would feel if next time you said "Hi, how are you doing? I hope today is going better for you." Everyone appreciates an employee with a good memory. This shows your customers that you value your relationship with them.

Memorize Customers' Names

When customers come into or call your business repeatedly, make it a point to recall their names. Addressing customers by name shows them that they are important to you. Repeating the name back to the customer will help you remember it. If the customer says, "This is Mr. Johnson. I'm calling about . . ." and you respond by saying "Yes, Mr. Johnson, I'll be happy to check on that," you show that you listened and acknowledged in a personal manner. If you do not know the customer well, always use the last name. "Hi, Mrs. Adams. How are you today?" Leave it up to Mrs. Adams to tell you whether you should call her by her first name.

TIP

To help remember names, repeat the person's name when you are introduced. "I'm pleased to meet you, Barbara." Use the name a couple of times during conversation: "Barbara, you mentioned that. . . ." After the person leaves, think of something that will help you remember the name. For example, you could create an associative memory jogger such as "Barbara, blue eyes."

Learn Your Customers' Preferences

Nothing will make customers feel better than to know you value them enough to know their likes (and even dislikes). This may be impossible if you handle a large number of customers; but if you are able, try to get to know your more frequent customers' preferences. Making notes on their account file may help jog your memory. "Hi, Mr. Jeffries. I'm glad you called. If I remember correctly, last time you called, the doodad you were looking for was out of stock. We just got some in." Better yet, if you remembered that Mr. Jeffries had been looking for a particular doodad and some just came in, why not call him? What a terrific way to cement your relationship!

Try to do something special every now and then for your repeat customers. It can be something as simple as taking the time to get to know them, showing new products that might interest them, or offering a special sale price on a product or service.

PICTURE THIS...

THE RIGHT WAY TO MAINTAIN ONGOING RELATIONSHIPS

The following week, Sarah spotted Beth in the store. She walked over to her. "Hi. I'm so glad you came in."

"You are?"

"I sure am. Today we got a shipment of the green skirt you were looking for. I thought of you and hoped you'd come in."

"That is great! I can't believe you remembered."

How Did the Customer Feel?

Beth was thrilled that Sarah remembered her and that she wanted a particular skirt. Sarah had built a relationship with Beth, and now she is working to maintain it. Next time Beth needs clothes, where do you think she will shop?

STEP 6
UNDERSTAND VARIOUS TYPES OF CUSTOMERS

Most of your customers will be pleasant people who are easy to satisfy. They come to you for help. You provide them with valid solutions and they are satisfied. But how do you handle those customers who are *not* pleasant and can be difficult to satisfy? They can test your patience and, in some cases, unhinge you. And what about customers who are culturally different or have disabilities that may make it difficult for you to communicate? When that happens, you are apt to feel uncomfortable because you are afraid you will say or do something wrong.

Below are some tips to help you interact successfully with people who can be difficult, along with those situations in which you find it difficult to know what to say and do.

The Pushy, Obnoxious, Agitated, Angry, or Demanding Customer—Remain Calm

When you stay calm, you stay in control. When you stay in control, you will be able to help this type of customer without coming unglued. Maintain a professional demeanor. Try to put the customer at ease. Speak softly and control your voice inflection. Never take on the same tone this type of customer uses with you. Speak in a positive, upbeat tone of voice. Keep a concerned or neutral facial expression. Remember, these types of behaviors may be ingrained. It may be part of their personalities, and perhaps acting in these manners is the only way they know how to act. In other words, do not take their behavior personally. They very well may act like this with everyone.

The Timid, Indecisive, Confused, or Stressed Customer—Be Patient

Help draw these customers out and get them to talk more. Ask open-ended questions. Listen closely to their responses and try to guide them to give you enough information to help them reach a decision. Some people are naturally shy. Some people have a difficult time reaching any decision. When people are stressed, they may find it tough to pay attention. Be sensitive to these types of customers and help them become more talkative by asking questions and encouraging them to talk. Guide them to make a decision based on the facts you are able to gather.

The Overly Friendly, Flirty, Wheeler-Dealer, or Melodramatic Customer—Be Professional

Keep your end of the conversation on business. These customers can be difficult to handle because they do not see their behavior as being out of line. It is up to you to control the conversation. Do not foster overly friendly or flirty behavior by being overly friendly in return. Guide your conversation back to business. If a flirty customer continues, offer a gentle reminder that you want to help—with a business solution. Try to rein in the wheeler-dealers by acting ethically. Be sensitive to those who love to be in the spotlight by focusing on the business interaction.

The Culturally Different Customer—Be Tolerant

We live in a society made up of many cultures, languages, and customs, yet people often do not know how to talk or act in the presence of a person from another culture. Projecting kindness, smiling, and being honest and sincere translate into any language and across any barrier. People who do not look like us or act like we do can make us uncomfortable. By learning to be tolerant of differences, you will overcome any cultural obstacles. If you have trouble understanding your customer's accent, ask him or her to repeat. Listen for key words. Ask questions to clarify. Keep your statements short. Check for understanding by summarizing the customer's request.

People with Disabilities—Be Respectful

Treat them like you treat anyone else. Make eye contact and speak in your normal tone and pace of speech. Focus on the person first and the disability second. Putting the disability first, such as saying "the handicapped person," places the focus on the disability rather than the person. When referring to a person with a disability, refer to the person first and use terms such as "the man who uses a wheelchair," "the woman who is blind," or "the person with epilepsy." Once you get used to dealing with people with disabilities, you will see that they want to be treated like anyone else, with dignity and respect.

TIP

If you do not know how to refer to a person, the proper term, when referring to someone who is handicapped, is to always put the person first, as in "person with a disability."

Here are some other suggestions as to how you should interact with people with disabilities:

■ Offer to shake hands if this is normally how you greet people. It is acceptable to shake a person's left hand. If, after offering your hand, you find the person is unable to shake hands, complete the handshake by placing your hand on the person's right hand.

■ Always ask first if a person wants help: "I'll be happy to reach that if you'd like."

■ If you don't know what to do to help a person, ask what you should do: "I'd like to help. Please tell me what I can do."

For people who use wheelchairs:

■ Try to place yourself at the person's eye level if you are going to have a lengthy conversation.

■ Never lean on a wheelchair or hover over the person.

■ Make eye contact and speak directly to the person, not to the person's companion.

For people with developmental or cognitive disabilities:

■ Speak clearly and use short, easy-to-understand words.

■ If the person has difficulty writing or typing, offer to help: "If you'd like, I'll be happy to complete the application for you."

■ Give the person ample time to formulate thoughts and respond to you.

■ Refrain from finishing the person's sentence.

For people with visual impairments:

■ Never touch a service dog without first asking permission.

- Tell the person about any obstacles in his or her path: "There are boxes in the aisle ahead, so we'll walk close to the wall."

- When asking the person to take a seat, help him or her touch the chair first.

- Verbalize what you are doing to help the person: "I'm inputting the information into my computer so I can give you an installation date."

For people with hearing impairments:

- Look at the person and speak and enunciate clearly.

- Keep your hands away from your face when speaking.

- Use simple words and short sentences.

For people with speech impairments:

- Ask the person to repeat if you do not understand; then repeat his/her words back to be sure you understood correctly.

- Use closed questions that require short answers.

TIP

In all cases, when interacting with people with disabilities, be patient. Also, don't be embarrassed or overly apologetic if you make a blunder.

When you learn to interact with different types of people and personalities, you will confidently handle any customer in any situation. By building and maintaining positive relationships, you are on your way to providing great customer service to every customer.

PICTURE THIS...
PUTTING IT ALL TOGETHER

After being trained, Sarah busied herself folding tops on the front display table.

Beth Adams, meanwhile, was outside the store looking at the clothing display in the window. She came into the store and noticed Sarah.

This was Sarah's first customer. She was nervous, but she knew what she needed to do. She looked at Beth, smiled, and said "Hi, how are you doing today?"

Beth smiled back. "I'm fine, thanks, how are you?"

"It's my first day, so I don't know yet. I'm a little nervous."

"I know how that feels. I'm sure you'll do just fine."

"If you need anything, I'll be happy to help you find it."

"Thanks, I'm looking for a skirt. I'll look around."

"Okay. We have skirts in great summer colors."

Beth smiled and walked away. Sarah continued to fold the tops while Beth browsed.

"Excuse me. Can you see if you have this skirt in a size twelve?" Beth asked.

Sarah took the skirt from Beth and said "Yes, I'll be happy to. I love this shade of green."

"I love it too. I hope you have it; I've been looking for a green skirt."

"I'll be right back." Sarah hurried into the stockroom. She came back with a different style green skirt and said "I'm sorry, we don't have that skirt in your size. I don't know if you saw this one. I brought it because you mentioned you wanted a green skirt."

"Thanks, but that isn't exactly what I was looking for."

"What type of skirt are you interested in?"

"I prefer longer skirts."

"What other colors would you be interested in?"

"I really wanted green, but I suppose I could use a khaki skirt."

"Do you care for prints?"

"No, I only wear solids."

"I'll check to see if we have the style you liked in khaki. I'll also see if we have other longer skirts in a solid green or khaki. I'll be right back."

"Thank you. That would be great."

Sarah returned with a skirt. "I found this khaki skirt. How do you like it?"

After looking it over, Beth said "Thanks for looking, but I still like the style of the green one better."

"I understand and I appreciate that you really liked that skirt. I hope next time you come in, we have the styles and colors you like."

The following week, Sarah spotted Beth in the store. She walked over to her. "Hi. I'm so glad you came in."

"You are?"

"I sure am. Today we got a shipment of the green skirt you were looking for. I thought of you and hoped you'd come in."

"That is great! I can't believe you remembered."

Your customer interactions may not always be this simple or straight-forward. Even if your customer contacts are much more involved, practice these steps and you will be able to build and maintain positive relationships with your customers.

Relationship Building Is the Cornerstone of Customer Service

As your company's representative—and the face of your business—your number-one job is to develop strong customer relationships, whether your customers do business with you repeatedly or are one-time visitors. When you make it your business to give each customer a positive experience, you demonstrate that you care and you show them they are important to you. Any relationship requires ongoing maintenance, including customer relationships. When you continually strive to strengthen these relationships, you build strong bonds that result in loyalty. Remember, your customers provide free advertising for you: Make sure that what they are saying about you is what you *want* said about you. When they say good things, you help your company retain and grow your business.

- Find ways to give them more than they expect.

- Tell your customers that you appreciate their business.

- Always make customers feel good about their interaction with you.

BUSINESS
N∅T
AS USUAL

KEY POINTS

Step 1: Establish Rapport

- Be friendly.
- Be interested.
- Be considerate.
- Find common ground.
- Be trustful.

Step 2: Interact Positively with Customers

- Be helpful.
- Be a problem solver.
- Be credible.
- Believe in your products.

Step 3: Identify Customers' Needs

- Ask questions.
- Summarize customers' needs.
- Recommend appropriate solutions.
- Handle objections.

Step 4: Make Each Customer Feel Valued

- Go out of your way for your customers.
- Validate customers' decisions.
- Instill positive feelings.

Step 5: Maintain Ongoing Relationships

- Remember your customers.
- Memorize customers' names.
- Learn your customers' preferences.

Step 6: Understand Various Types of Customers

■ Pushy, obnoxious, agitated, angry, or demanding customers—
  remain calm.

■ Timid, indecisive, confused, or stressed customers—be patient.

■ Overly friendly, flirty, wheeler-dealer, or melodramatic customers—
  be professional.

■ Culturally different customers—be tolerant.

■ People with disabilities—be respectful.

P R A C T I C E   L E S S O N

Step 1: Establish Rapport

Think of your typical customers. How can you begin establishing rapport?

_____

_____

Step 2: Interact Positively with Customers

What are some ways in which you can interact positively with your typical customer?

_____

_____

Step 3: Identify Customers' Needs

What questions can you ask to uncover your typical customers' needs?

_____

_____

Step 4: Make the Customer Feel Valued

What are some things you can say at the end of the interaction to make your customers feel valued?

_____

_____

Step 5: Maintain Ongoing Relationships

What are some things you can do to make your repeat customers feel special?

_____

_____

Step 6: Handle Various Types of Customers

Think about a recent customer listed below. What did you do right? What could you have done better?

Agitated

_____

_____

Confused

_____

_____

Wheeler-dealer

_____

_____

Culturally different

_____

_____

Disabled

_____

_____

D O I N G   I T   R I G H T !

You may not be old enough to remember the television show *Cheers*, about a neighborhood bar where the "regulars" gathered every night. At *Cheers*, the regulars, the employees, and the owner were like a big extended family. When you think about it, aren't those the types of places you like to go? The places where they always know your name and they're always glad you came?

When it comes to restaurants, I'm fortunate to live in an area where we have many from which to choose. One of my favorites is Sal's Pizzeria. The first time my husband and I walked into his restaurant, Sal paused momentarily from tossing pizza dough to greet us warmly: "Hi, folks. Thanks for coming in."

His wait staff was equally warm and friendly, smiling and talking with the diners. Clearly, this was a place where Sal and his employees enjoyed coming to work. During our meal, Sal walked from table to table, talking to all the diners. We chatted a few minutes, and my husband and Sal, both being from New Jersey, talked about things they had in common.

The second time we went to Sal's, he paused from tossing pizza dough. "Hey, New Jersey!" he called out. With all the customers coming through his door, I thought it was great that Sal not only remembered us, he remembered something about us.

Since that second visit we have become regulars at Sal's. It meant a lot that he took the time to get to know us and build a relationship. The hostess also knows us, and if she hasn't seen us in a while, she will ask how we've been. Our usual server remembers what we like to drink and what we normally order. Order something different? She's likely to say "Not going with the usual tonight?" Everyone at Sal's makes us feel like we are part of their family.

Building relationships is important in any business. Taking the time to get to know your customers is a giant first step in building relationships. After all, we do want to go where everybody knows our names, and they're always glad we came. When you welcome customers into your business and treat them like family, they'll become like family—loyal to you.

H O W   D O   I   M E A S U R E   U P ?

In my place of employment:

1. Who are my customers?

   _____

   _____

2. What do they expect from our business?

   _____

   _____

3. How do our products and services enhance their lives?

   _____

   _____

4. How can I use these answers to establish a relationship with my customers?

   _____

   _____

II

PUTTING YOUR
CUSTOMERS FIRST

CHAPTER

4

Seeing Eye to Eye:
Face-to-Face Contacts

**CUSTOMERS COME INTO A BUSINESS BECAUSE OF THE PRODUCTS
BUT COME AGAIN ONLY WHEN THEY RECEIVE GREAT SERVICE**

Write down a typical customer contact that is reflective of your face-to-face interactions:

_____

_____

_____

_____

_____

_____

Think about this scenario as you work through this chapter. Use it as the example when answering the Practice Lesson questions at the end of the chapter.

Providing exceptional customer service is not that difficult when you have the necessary skills, such as displaying courteous and respectful behaviors, communicating effectively, and building relationships with your customers. In this, and the following chapters in Part II, you will put these skills to work by learning the three steps of customer service for various types of interactions.

CUSTOMER SERVICE IS FACE-TO-FACE CONTACTS

You have already learned that creating a positive first impression will help you build the foundation for providing great customer service. Customers are going to judge you by your initial look, manner, and actions. Did you know that customers also get a first impression of your overall business when they come in? In addition to forming a first impression of you, your customers also judge your place of business by its look, image, and overall atmosphere.

Giving exceptional face-to-face customer service begins when your customers enter your place of business. From the moment a customer walks through your door, you have the opportunity to offer a warm and inviting welcome. That welcome includes what you say and what your customer sees. Helping customers by showing them where to find items, answering questions, finding the right solutions, and making sure they are satisfied before leaving will ensure that your customers feel appreciated and valued.

Their assessment, particularly when they are forming that crucial first impression, includes how you look and act, how your business looks and feels, and how well you interact with them. Customers may come to your business for a product or service, but they will decide to stay or leave based on an overall feeling of warmth or coolness.

Think of a business you went into recently. What was your first impression? Did you feel welcomed, or did you feel so uncomfortable that you could not wait to leave? If the business made you feel welcome:

■ *What did the employees do that made you feel welcome?*

■ *What aspects of the business's appearance made you feel welcome?*

If the business made you feel uncomfortable:

■ *What did the employees do that made you feel uncomfortable?*

■ *What aspects of the business's appearance made you feel uncomfortable?*

Now think about the image your place of business presents to your customers. Mentally walk through your business from a customer's viewpoint. Start by walking through the front door. Take a good look at what your customers see.

Envision your business as if you are seeing it for the first time. Look at the colors, decorations, cleanliness, and neatness.

■ *What do your customers see when they first step into your business?*

■ *How easy is it to move about?*

■ *How accessible are your display areas?*

■ *Is there a sensible traffic flow pattern?*

■ *Is the lighting sufficient?*

■ *Is everything clean, including bathrooms?*

Pay close attention to all details—your customers will. As a group, try to come up with ideas to improve the overall look and image of your business. Think about color, function, and feel. Here are some things to pay attention to:

■ Try to create a focal point for customers when they enter your business, whether it's an interesting piece of furniture, a piece of artwork, or an interesting display case. Create something that is memorable.

■ Decorate your business in a style that suits the image you are trying to project. Knowing who your customers are is important when creating the appropriate look and feel.

■ Pay close attention to cleanliness and organization. Even if your business is decorated to suit your customers, it will not hold their attention if they first see clutter or a dirty appearance.

■ Remember to focus on your own image. Think about the total package you present: your courtesy, attitude, appearance, manner of speaking, nonverbal signals, listening skills, interest, and ability to build strong relationships.

PICTURE THIS...
THE WRONG WAY TO GIVE FACE-TO-FACE CUSTOMER SERVICE

Dave Benjamin had an appointment for a physical examination. He arrived at the physician's office, feeling slightly uneasy because it was his first appointment with this doctor. He walked into the office, looked around at the bland beige walls, the row of industrial-looking chairs, a table with ripped magazines strewn about, and the drab brown carpeting. Two other people were waiting. He eyed a sliding window with a note taped on it: "Please sign in. We will call you when we're ready for you." He signed his name on the pad and took a seat. Someone on the other side of the window slid the window open, looked at his name, and quickly shut the window without saying a word. He sat, anxiously waiting, wondering when his name would be called.

The window slid open again. "Mr. Benjamin?"

Dave sprang up and walked quickly to the window.

"You need to fill out this form since you haven't been here before," a woman said, no expression in her voice, as she handed him a clipboard. "When you're done, leave it on the ledge."

Dave completed the paperwork and placed it on the ledge. The woman slid the window open, took the clipboard, and then shut the window. After the other two people were called, Dave waited for what seemed an eternity. A nurse finally called his name. "Mr. Benjamin?" He walked toward her. "Follow me. I need to weigh you and take your blood pressure."

What Went Wrong?

Presenting a positive business personality would have meant a lot to Dave. Bland beige walls, the row of uncomfortable chairs, the table with ripped magazines, the drab brown carpeting, and the employee behind the glass wall all sent a negative message about the office environment. The employee who sat behind the wall also sent a negative message that she was not approachable. Neither she, nor the nurse, made Dave feel welcome.

How Did the Customer Feel?

Dave formed a poor first impression. Because this was his first visit, he had entered the office feeling uncomfortable. When he noticed the appearance of the waiting room, he felt that the doctor and the employees were not concerned about the way the office looked. When the receptionist did not say hello and just handed him the clipboard, he felt even more uncomfortable. And finally, when the nurse came for him, she did nothing to put him at ease.

A customer's first impression is based on both the employees and the overall atmosphere of the company. A company can have a messy appearance and great employees. Likewise, a company may have a great appearance and employees with terrible attitudes. It pays off when you have both: a pleasant business appearance and caring employees.

Giving exceptional customer service, when dealing with customers in person, seems pretty simple on face value. And it is, when you break down your interactions into three steps that must be completed for a successful outcome. Learn the following, and you will be on your way to providing exceptional face-to-face customer service:

Step 1: Welcome Your Customers

Step 2: Find the Best Solutions

Step 3: Show Appreciation

In Dave's situation, his discomfort would have been eased if he had walked into a clean, well decorated, organized waiting room. He would have felt much better if the receptionist had talked to him. When the nurse came for him, she could have smiled and made small talk to make him feel comfortable.

STEP 1

WELCOME YOUR CUSTOMERS

Giving exceptional face-to-face service begins when your customers enter your door. They expect to be welcomed into your business. In Chapter 1, you learned the importance of making a good first impression and how that can set the stage for the entire interaction. There will be occasions, though, when no matter how hard you try, you cannot accomplish this. You might remind a customer of her old boyfriend. You might remind a customer of his rude neighbor. A customer might not like the way you look for no rational reason. Therefore, welcoming your customers into your place of business can enhance a first impression. When you demonstrate that you are happy to help, customers are more apt to view you positively and feel comfortable with you.

Greet Every Customer

A quick smile, an interested facial expression, and a friendly greeting all send a message to your customers that they are number one with you and that you are genuinely happy they chose your business. A friendly greeting will help overcome any negative vibes that customers may pick up when they are forming their first impressions.

Make an Impressionable Opening Statement

What you say is important in presenting yourself well to your customers. When you greet them, say more than just "hello." Add something to let them know you are happy they walked through your door. Try something like: "Hi, welcome to Karen's Bakery," or "Good morning. We're glad you came in." When you say more than just hello, you are really saying that you are interested in them and you appreciate their choosing your business. If you remember a customer from a previous visit, acknowledge him or her differently, for example, "Hello. It's great to see you again." Address him or her by name if you know it: "Hi, Juanita, how are you doing today?"

Ask How You Can Help, and Give Your Name

After greeting your customers and making an impressionable opening statement, ask how you can help. Even if you work in an establishment where your customers come in to browse, let them know you are there if they need your assistance. You might say "Are you looking for anything particular today?" or "My name is Jody, and I'll be happy to help you in any way." In the doctor's office, the receptionist could have assured Dave that she would help if he had any questions about the form he had been asked to fill out. Since this was his first visit, talking to him, explaining the process, and asking if he had any questions would have put him at ease.

Tune In to Your Customers

Pay close attention to customers' nonverbal signals. Make eye contact and smile at them. Watch to see if they quickly and easily smile back. If not, try to pick up on emotional cues. Pay attention to their attitudes. When you are interested in your customers, you will be able to pick up on their moods and emotions, and you can respond accordingly. It should have been fairly evident that Dave was uncomfortable. Had the receptionist tuned in to Dave's actions and demeanor, she could have said something positive to ease his discomfort.

PICTURE THIS...
THE RIGHT WAY TO GREET CUSTOMERS

Dave Benjamin arrived at the physician's office, feeling slightly uneasy because it was his first appointment with this doctor. He walked into the office, looked around at warm butterscotch walls, an interesting grouping of chairs, a table with magazines neatly organized, and an Oriental rug covering the wood floors.

He saw an open sliding window. A cheerful woman smiled and greeted him. "Good morning. How are you today?"

"I'm fine, thank you. I'm Dave Benjamin. I have an appointment with Dr. Gilbert."

"Thank you, Mr. Benjamin. Since this is your first time seeing Dr. Gilbert, will you please complete this new-patient information form?" She reviewed the form with Dave. "When you complete it, you can bring it back to me. My name is Kathy, and if you have any questions I'll be happy to help you." Sensing his discomfort, she smiled warmly.

Dave completed the form and returned it to Kathy.

She quickly looked it over. "Thanks, Mr. Benjamin. Have a seat, and Dr. Gilbert's nurse will call you. It shouldn't take long."

How Did the Customer Feel?

When Kathy warmly greeted Dave, she gave him her full attention. She projected a confident, caring attitude that made Dave feel that she was interested in him. Tuning in to his feelings, Kathy sensed that he felt uneasy, so she made it a point to offer to help him in any way she could, assuring him he would not have to wait long. Dave's first impression was positive, and he felt less tense.

STEP 2
FIND THE BEST SOLUTIONS

After greeting your customers, it is time to get to the nuts and bolts of helping them. They came to you for a reason. Finding out that reason and finding the best solution is your next step in helping your customers. Remember to pay attention to that one customer—and *only* that one customer. Show you are interested in helping by listening attentively and by making eye contact. When you are helping a customer, shut out internal and external distractions so you can stay focused.

TIP

> If a phone call comes in while you are helping a customer, ask the caller to hold while you finish, or offer to call back. Never make the customer, who is ready to do business, wait while you take a call.

Effectiveness and Efficiency Are Important

Being effective means finding the right solution, and the only way you can do that is to know your products, services, and company policies. Learn all you can about what your business has to offer. If you are unsure about a customer's needs, ask your manager or a coworker to help find the right product or service. Being efficient means finding the best solution quickly. You can be knowledgeable; but if you take too long to come up with a recommendation or find a solution, you are going to lose ground with your customers. Customers value employees who are both effective and efficient.

Show and Tell

When a customer asks where something is located, show him or her rather than pointing or telling where it is. Walk the customer to that area of the business. If it is a small item, pick it up and hand it to the customer. Ask if the customer has any questions and, if so, offer a complete description, including the benefits of the product.

Make the Most of Your Question-and-Answer Period

When you offer to help and the customer asks for a specific item, show the item to him or her and then ask questions to make sure it is the best product for the customer's needs. Use a combination of open and closed questions to learn more and make a recommendation based on what he or she tells you.

Know When to Stay and When to Go

Pick up on your customer's cues as to whether he or she wants you to stay and help, or would prefer to be left alone. Sometimes people come in to browse, or perhaps they are unsure of what solution they are looking for. Do not be overbearing. If they want time to look around, say "Please take your time. I'll be right here if I can help you," or "I'll be happy to help if you need anything."

Find the Right Solution

When you are knowledgeable about your products and services, you will present yourself confidently. Your customers will trust that you have done your best to find the right solution, and they will feel good about coming to you for help. Remember, though, that one size never fits all. Flexibility is important when dealing with different types of customers, scenarios, and specific needs. That is the only sure way you can give each customer individualized service.

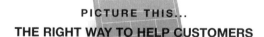

PICTURE THIS...
THE RIGHT WAY TO HELP CUSTOMERS

Soon a nurse came into the waiting room. "Mr. Benjamin?" Dave walked toward her. She said, "My name is Ann. How are you doing?"

"I'm fine, thanks."

"Great. Come with me, I'll get you weighed and take your blood pressure first. Then Dr. Gilbert will see you."

How Did the Customer Feel?

By the time Ann came for him, Dave felt comfortable being in Dr. Gilbert's office. Both Kathy and Ann had explained the procedures to Dave. Because Dave was comfortable with the employees, with the look of the office, and with the organized manner in which it was run, Dave felt he was in good hands.

STEP 3
SHOW APPRECIATION

Customers are going to remember something about their visit. Whether they do business with you or not, you should always make their visit memorable by making them feel appreciated.

Gain the Customer's Agreement

Rather than assuming that the customer buys in to your suggestions, always confirm first: "How does this sound to you?" If the customer agrees, complete the request. In the event that you were not able to find a workable solution, the customer will know that you tried your best.

Make Sure the Customer Is Satisfied

When you have asked the right questions and answered the questions correctly, when you have identified the customer's needs, and when you have found the best solution for them, go one step further to make sure the customer is satisfied with the solution. If you know the customer is happy, validate his or her decision by adding an assurance: "I'm sure you'll be happy with that choice. It's one of our most popular items." If you feel the customer may be hesitant or unsure, ask something like "Do you have any questions about how this works?" If you were unable to find the right solution, say "I'm sorry we didn't have the _____ you were looking for." As for the browsing customer who leaves without doing business, you might ask, "Was there something specific you were looking for?"

Acknowledge Customers for Coming in to Your Business

Always let your customers know that you appreciate their business by saying something such as "I enjoyed helping you today" or "I'm glad I could resolve your billing problem." If he or she does not do business with you, say "Thank you for coming in" or "Thanks for stopping in. Next time I hope we have what you're looking for." Let your customers know you hope to see them again by saying "We look forward to seeing you soon." When you are confident that you have handled your customers to the best of your ability, showing appreciation in a heartfelt, sincere manner will leave a positive lasting impression in your customers' minds.

PICTURE THIS...
THE RIGHT WAY TO END YOUR CONTACTS

Dr. Gilbert completed Dave's physical. "Mr. Benjamin, it looks like you are taking great care of yourself. Do you have any questions?"

"I can't think of any."

"After you finish dressing, please stop at the reception area and they'll finish your paperwork. Unless something changes and you need to come in, I'll see you in a year. It was a pleasure meeting you." Dr. Gilbert smiled, shook Dave's hand, and said good-bye.

Kathy saw him coming. "Mr. Benjamin, I have your paperwork right here. Do you have any questions?"

"No, Dr. Gilbert was great. She spent a lot of time with me. I'm glad I came to see her."

"That's nice to hear. Would you like us to mail you a reminder card for your next appointment?"

"No, that's okay. I'll remember to call."

"We do get booked up quickly, so please try to call about two months prior so we can schedule a convenient appointment."

"Thanks for letting me know. I'll make sure I do that."

"Thank you, and have a great day."

How Did the Customer Feel?

Kathy ended on a positive note by asking if Dave had any questions. His answer told her that he was satisfied with his interaction with Dr. Gilbert. She ended by explaining the scheduling procedure and then thanking him.

The following week, one of Dave's coworkers asked if anyone knew of a good doctor. "I do," Dave answered. "I just saw Dr. Gilbert last week for a physical. She was great. Besides that, the office is clean, the staff is very friendly, and they went out of their way to make me feel comfortable. I'd definitely recommend her."

Whenever you are a customer and go into a business, pay close attention to the way you are treated. Think about the things you liked and the things you did not like. Learn from watching others. Make sure you treat customers the way you like to be treated.

PICTURE THIS...
PUTTING IT ALL TOGETHER

Dave Benjamin arrived at the physician's office, feeling slightly uneasy because it was his first appointment with this doctor. He walked into the office and looked around at warm butterscotch walls, an interesting grouping of chairs, a table with magazines neatly organized, and an Oriental rug covering the wood floors.

He saw an open sliding glass window. A cheerful woman smiled and greeted him. "Good morning. How are you today?"

"I'm fine, thank you. I'm Dave Benjamin. I have an appointment with Dr. Gilbert."

"Thank you, Mr. Benjamin. Since this is your first time seeing Dr. Gilbert, will you please complete this new-patient information form?" She reviewed the form with Dave. "When you complete it, you can bring it back to me. My name is Kathy, and if you have any questions I'll be happy to help you." Sensing his discomfort, she smiled warmly.

Dave completed the form and returned it to Kathy.

She quickly looked it over. "Thanks, Mr. Benjamin. Have a seat, and Dr. Gilbert's nurse will call you. It shouldn't take long."

Soon a nurse came into the waiting room. "Mr. Benjamin?" Dave walked toward her. She said "My name is Ann. How are you doing?"

"I'm fine, thanks."

"Great. Come with me, I'll get you weighed and take your blood pressure first. Then Dr. Gilbert will see you."

Dr. Gilbert completed Dave's physical. "Mr. Benjamin, it looks like you are taking great care of yourself. Do you have any questions?"

"I can't think of any."

"After you finish dressing, please stop at the reception area and they'll finish your paperwork. Unless something changes and you need to come in, I'll see you in a year. It was a pleasure meeting you." Dr. Gilbert smiled, shook Dave's hand, and said good-bye.

Kathy saw him coming. "Mr. Benjamin, I have your paperwork right here. Do you have any questions?"

"No, Dr. Gilbert was great. She spent a lot of time with me. I'm glad I came to see her."

"That's nice to hear. Would you like us to mail you a reminder card for your next appointment?"

"No, that's okay. I'll remember to call."

"We do get booked up quickly, so please try to call about two months prior so we can schedule a convenient appointment."

"Thanks for letting me know. I'll make sure I do that."

"Thank you, and have a great day."

Although you may not automatically think of a physician's office as a customer service provider, every business provides customer service. It is important that anyone—in any business—who interacts with customers understands this. Customers, even patients, will go to someone else if they are not satisfied with their treatment.

Customers Come into a Business Because of the Products, but Come Again Only When They Receive Great Service

Consumer confidence ranks poorly across the board. Customers have become more cynical when it comes to business dealings. They have been accustomed to being treated poorly by frontline employees and even management, and are—rightfully so—selective about where they spend their cash. Never take your customers for granted. Treat them poorly? They will leave as fast as they came in. Not interested in finding a workable solution? They will find a business that is interested.

Getting customers into your brick-and-mortar business may be a little tougher now with so many online shopping choices; so when customers come in, make sure you do everything you can to satisfy their requests. It really isn't that difficult:

- Welcome your customers into your business. Immediately begin building a relationship by establishing rapport.

- Find the best solution for each customer. Communicate well by asking questions, answering questions, and, most important, listening well.

- Show appreciation. Use basic courtesies such as saying "Thank you for coming in."

When you demonstrate to your customers that you want their business, you send a powerful message that you are going to do all you can to keep their business. When you do that, you increase your chances of staying in business.

KEY POINTS

Step 1: Welcome Your Customers

- Greet every customer.
- Make an impressionable opening statement.

- Ask how you can help, and give your name.
- Tune in to your customers.

Step 2: Find the Best Solutions

- Effectiveness and efficiency are important.
- Show and tell.
- Make the most of your question-and-answer period.
- Know when to stay and when to go.
- Find the right solution.

Step 3: Show Appreciation

- Gain the customer's agreement.
- Make sure the customer is satisfied.
- Acknowledge customers for coming in to your business.

PRACTICE LESSON

Refer to the customer contact example you wrote down at the beginning of the chapter.

Step 1: Welcome Your Customers

Offer a welcoming statement.

_____

_____

Step 2: Find the Best Solutions

What are the general steps you are going to take to help your typical customer?

_____

_____

Step 3: Show Appreciation

What will you say to the customer you helped to show your appreciation?

_____

_____

What will you say to a customer for whom you could not find the right solution?

_____

_____

_____

D O I N G   I T   R I G H T !

I bet if you asked a hundred people to list their favorite pastimes, not one would list grocery shopping among their top ten. It just happens to be one of those necessary tasks in life. We eat; therefore, we grocery shop.

Grocery store managers understand this fact. They know we will come. Why, then, should grocery stores care about customer service?

The truth is that many *don't* seem to care. You've probably been to stores where the parking lot is littered with shopping carts, employees bury themselves in their work, shelves are sometimes empty, the cashier grumbles a disinterested greeting, you have to bag your own groceries— or worse, get stuck with the bagger who throws the heavy items on top of the light ones. Or upside down. You leave the store with your groceries, but not with a positive feeling.

It's not that way at the grocery store where I shop. Providing exceptional customer service is their number-one goal. Daryl, the store manager, his department and assistant managers, and the employees actively demonstrate that they care about their customers.

Daryl can usually be found not in his office but walking around the store, pitching in to help when needed. His department and assistant managers are where they should be: in their respective departments, on the floor, always close at hand.

Daryl and his management team take care of all the little details that add up to a positive shopping experience. Carts are rounded up frequently. If you need help, an employee is always nearby. Employees are constantly stocking shelves. The cashiers are friendly and will chat as they scan. And don't even think about bagging your own groceries. Every time I try, a manager sends someone right over—and the groceries are bagged correctly.

Customer service really begins with setting expectations—if Daryl didn't care, his employees wouldn't. If he wasn't a hands-on manager, his department and assistant managers wouldn't be hands-on either. He sets high customer service expectations and, most important, because he walks the talk, his employees walk the talk.

You see, even a chore such as grocery shopping can turn into a pleasant experience when the managers and employees genuinely care for their customers. When your customers have to do business with you— why not do what you can to make their experience pleasurable? Think about it this way: Doing everything you can to make your customers feel good makes you feel good. Knowing you did your best is always satisfying.

H O W   D O   I   M E A S U R E   U P ?

1. When I greet my customers, do I show enthusiasm and interest? What standard greeting can I use for new customers? What can I say and do to welcome my customers?

   _____

   _____

_____

_____

2. How effective and efficient am I in helping customers? What technical skills do I need to learn? Do I always remember to show and tell and ask questions to make sure the customer finds the best solution? If not, what internal cues can I teach myself to do better?

_____

_____

_____

_____

3. Do I make sure all my customers are satisfied, whether or not they do business with us? How can I improve in this area?

_____

_____

_____

_____

CHAPTER

Saying It with a Smile:
Telephone Contacts

AS YOUR COMPANY'S VOICE,
ALWAYS REPRESENT YOUR COMPANY WELL

Write down a typical customer exchange that reflects your telephone contacts:

_____

_____

_____

_____

_____

_____

Think about the scenario you have created as you work through this chapter. Use it as the example when answering the Practice Lesson questions at the end of the chapter.

If your job is to handle customer contacts by telephone, then you understand that this requires a different skill set than dealing with customers in person. Listening becomes even more important when you cannot see your customers. If you do not listen completely, you will not have the benefit of picking up on nonverbal cues and signals and you may miss important details. When customers cannot see you, what you say, how you say it, and what you do not say all are extremely important.

CUSTOMER SERVICE IS TELEPHONE CONTACTS

Answering promptly and greeting your customers with enthusiasm and a helpful attitude gets you off to a good start. Maintain a professional and friendly telephone demeanor. Assure customers that you can help. Keep an ongoing dialogue. Ask appropriate questions. Respond correctly. Recap the actions you are going to take. Doing these things communicates to your customers that you are interested in providing excellent service, and they will feel confident that you handled their requests correctly. Finally, thanking customers for doing business with you leaves them with a good feeling about calling your place of business.

BRAINSTORM

Think about some businesses you have called recently. What was your impression of your phone contacts?

In your phone contacts that were positive experiences, what did the employee say and do that made you feel comfortable?

In your phone contacts that were negative experiences, what did the employee say and do that caused you to feel uncomfortable?

Now think about your own place of business. Think about how you and your coworkers respond to customers when they call. Work through a mental phone call from start to finish and ask yourself the following questions:

- *Do you handle contacts in a manner that makes customers feel good about calling your company?*

- *When you answer calls, how do you greet customers and welcome them 'into' your business?*

- *What do you say to assure customers that you will help them?*

- *While you are handling phone requests, what do you say or ask to make your customers comfortable?*

- *If you called your company, how would you feel?*

Focus on all aspects of the phone contact, because your customers are going to. As a group, discuss ways in which you can make your phone customers feel as though they are walking through your door rather than calling you on the phone. Finding ways to make them feel welcome is your main goal in this exercise.

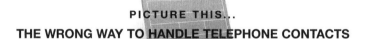

PICTURE THIS...
THE WRONG WAY TO HANDLE TELEPHONE CONTACTS

Diane Parker likes the convenience of shopping by catalog. When she had trouble placing an online order, she called the company's toll-free number. Ashley works in the catalog call center, where her job is to take orders from customers. When she received the call from Diane, the interaction went like this:

"VeeJay's Sportswear."

"Hi. I had trouble placing an order online. Can you take the order for me?"

"Yes, I can. May I have your name and billing address?"

"Diane Parker. My address is 23 Sycamore Road. . . ."

"Is that the address where you want your order shipped?"

"Yes."

"What is your first catalog number?"

"14236."

"Size?"

"Medium."

"Color?"

"Rose."

"Next item?"

Diane continued to give her list of items, along with her credit card information. Then there was silence on the other end of the line. Diane waited. And waited. She began to wonder what was happening. Had the employee put her on hold? Had she forgotten about her? Had she taken a break? "Hello," she said into the silence.

"I'm here," came a bland reply. "I'm waiting for your order to process. It shouldn't be long."

Diane waited again.

"Your order has gone through. All items are in stock and will be shipped out tomorrow. Is there anything else I can help you with?"

"No, thanks."

"Thank you for calling."

Diane hung up, hoping Ashley had gotten all the items correct.

What Went Wrong?

Ashley was efficient in taking Diane's order. She most likely followed her company's instructions as to how catalog orders should be taken. But it sounded as though Diane was giving her order to an automated system. Ashley added nothing to her interaction with Diane. While Ashley may have technically handled the order process correctly, she left out the important detail of putting a personal touch into the contact. It is this personal touch in your phone conversations that will make you come alive in an interaction with a customer.

How Did the Customer Feel?

Because Ashley did nothing to establish rapport, Diane felt blasé about their interaction. When Ashley did not recap the order, Diane wondered if she had input all the items correctly. She did not end up with a warm feeling about this company.

When you deal with customers on the telephone, your verbal communication skills—particularly the tone of your voice—are important. Whether your attitude is tinged with enthusiasm, sarcasm, boredom, or disinterest, your customers will hear you—loudly and clearly. Make sure the attitude you convey is that you are enthusiastic about helping them.

Learn the following steps, and you will give exceptional customer service to your telephone customers.

Step 1: Welcome Your Customers

Step 2: Find the Best Solutions

Step 3: Show Appreciation

In Diane's phone call, Ashley could have shown more enthusiasm by answering the call: "Thank you for calling VeeJay's. How may I help you today?" She could have interacted more throughout the contact. For example, she could have repeated the item name when Diane gave the number: "Item 14236, the denim jacket. What size and color would you like that in?" Small verbalizations like these can make a big difference with telephone customers.

TIP

Putting Your Best Ear Forward: Listening Attentively
When you communicate with another person face to face, you may be able to fudge if you do not listen completely. You can pick up cues by paying attention to a person's body language and facial expressions. You may even be able to drift off and still pick up somewhere in the middle of the conversation by going with the flow and observing the other person's actions as he or she speaks.

This is not so when you are on the phone. When you cannot see the other person, your only means of communication is the give and take of listening and talking. The most important component of good telephone communication is the ability to shut out all distractions and listen attentively so that you are able to respond appropriately.

STEP 1
WELCOME YOUR CUSTOMERS

The first few moments of your telephone conversation can set the tone for the entire contact, beginning with the manner in which you answer the call. You either welcome customers into your business, or, like Ashley in the example, make customers wonder why they called.

Answer Promptly

When customers call your business, they expect the phone to be answered quickly. If your company employs an automated answering system, customers expect to be able to move through the prompts and reach a live person without delay. If you allow your phone to ring or if your call answering system is lengthy or confusing, your customers may opt out and call another business that provides more efficient phone answering.

Give the Name of Your Business, Your Name, and an Opening Statement or Question

When giving your opening statement or question, sound enthusiastic and ready to help. Speak in a professional, yet friendly, tone. If your company requires you to answer with a standard greeting, practice saying it so that you do not sound mechanical or robotic. It may help to speak in your natural voice as though you are greeting a friend.

TIP

When speaking to a customer on the phone, never chew gum or eat. You might think the person on the other end will not hear it, but you may be wrong.

PICTURE THIS...

THE RIGHT WAY TO BEGIN TELEPHONE CONTACTS

"Thank you for calling VeeJay's Sportswear. My name is Ashley. How may I help you today?"

"Hi. I had trouble placing an order online. Can you take the order for me?"

"I'm sorry you had trouble. I'll be glad to take your order."

How Did the Customer Feel?

Ashley was ready to handle the call when she answered. She gave the name of the business and her own name, and she asked how she could help. Diane picked up on Ashley's enthusiasm and willingness to be of assistance.

STEP 2

FIND THE BEST SOLUTIONS

Between hello and good-bye, you have the opportunity to handle customers' requests in a manner that either leaves them feeling good about calling your company, or makes them wonder why they bothered calling. You are your company's voice; how you handle each customer's request is how the customer is going to remember your company.

Give Your Full Attention

If you do not pay attention from the moment you answer the phone, you will make a poor first impression. Asking a customer to repeat the opening statement or asking a customer to hold a moment while you finish something is not the right way to begin your conversation. When that happens, you will need to work harder to establish rapport and earn the customer's trust. Always start your phone contacts on a positive note by being ready to listen and ready to help. When you pay attention and listen to the reason for the call, you can begin finding the best solution for that customer.

Summarize the Customer's Opening Statement

Before you attempt to handle a customer's request, make sure you understand what he or she wants. Recap what the customer said without repeating it verbatim. You could say, "You received a blue jacket instead of the white one that you ordered?" This way, the customer will clear up any confusion before you go on: "No, I received a white jacket but I wanted blue." If you feel sure you understood correctly, incorporate the summary into your assurance statement: "I'm sorry that happened. I'll be happy to look into why we sent you a blue jacket when you ordered white."

Verbalize What You Are Doing

Explain to your customer what you are doing throughout the contact. Never assume that the person on the other end understands. "I'm waiting for your order to process, and then I can give you the confirmation number." If you need to ask a series of questions, explain what you will be doing so the customer does not think you are interrogating: "I'm going to need some additional information to help you. Do you have your invoice handy?" Now, when you begin asking questions, the customer understands what you are doing.

During Pauses, Tell the Customer What Is Happening

There are instances in which you will need to pause your conversation with a customer. Silence, to a customer on the other end of a phone line, can create confusion: Are you still there? What are you doing? Letting them know you are still there and working builds trust. For example, you might need to read notes from previous contacts or wait for a response from an employee in another department, or you are a new employee and need to give your full attention to completing the request. Let the customer know why there is a pause in your conversation. For example, "I need to read the comments from your previous conversation, as that will help me know what's been done. I'll stay on the line with you, though."

Put Your Personal Touch into the Contact

You can maintain professionalism and still show your human side. Talk to the customer while you are waiting for a computer screen to change: "It'll be just a moment for the next screen. How are you doing today?" or "Our computer system is running a little slow right now. Could be because it's freezing cold here!" When you put a personal touch into your contacts, you will be able to establish rapport and possibly find common ground. Your customer may respond "That's why we moved to Florida. It's sunny and in the seventies here." Weather is usually a great topic on which to find common ground.

TIP

> If you are a new employee, it is all right to say so. Doing so may help you build rapport with your customers. Everyone has been new at a job, and customers will relate and be patient with you. You can say something like "I really appreciate your patience. I'm new here, and I want to make sure I input everything correctly for you."

Explain Why You Need to Place Customers on Hold

Explaining why you are going to put a customer on hold is a common courtesy that will be appreciated: "I'll need to place you on hold so I can find out why your order's been delayed." In addition, be sure to tell your customer approximately how long it will take: "It may take me a few minutes to get the information I need." If you place a customer on hold and then find it is taking longer than you thought, return to the line and offer an update: "Mr. Perkins, I'm still waiting for my technician to give me an answer. It shouldn't take that much longer." If the wait time will be extremely long, offer to call the customer back and make a specific commitment: "I'll get back to you by five o'clock today with the information."

BRAINSTORM

> If your job requires you to make outgoing phone contacts or cold calls for sales, as a group create an outline for handling this type of call. Include all aspects of your contact in your script:

- Greeting—introducing yourself and your company

- Explaining the reason for your call

- Questions you will ask

Role-play to practice your message before making outgoing calls. And remember that this "script" is a framework only. Flexibility helps you put your personality into the conversation.

PICTURE THIS...
THE RIGHT WAY TO HELP TELEPHONE CUSTOMERS

"May I have your name and your billing address?"

"Sure. It's Diane Parker. My address is 23 Sycamore Road. . . ."

"Is that the address where you want your order shipped?"

"Yes."

"It'll take just a minute for my screen to change. How are you doing today?"

"I'm great. How are you?"

"I'm doing well, thank you. Hmm, our system seems to be a little slow this morning, but the screen should come right up." After a short pause, Ashley said, "Here we go. I'm ready to take your order now. What is your first catalog number?"

"SU-14236."

"That's the misses' denim jacket. What size and color would you like?"

"Size medium in rose."

"I have the same jacket, and it's really comfortable. What is the next item number?"

"SU-14707."

"Denim slacks. Size and color?"

"Size ten in rose."

"All right. Next?"

Ashley input all the information, adding a personal touch from time to time until Diane finished.

"Thank you. It'll take a moment for the order to process and then I'll give you your order number."

How Did the Customer Feel?

Diane felt comfortable during the phone call. Ashley was ready to take her order, and she verbalized what she was doing throughout the contact. Before pauses, Ashley explained the reason for the delay. She built a relationship throughout the contact by being friendly yet professional, and that came across to Diane.

STEP 3
SHOW APPRECIATION

Learning how to effectively handle telephone interactions begins when you answer, continues when you take care of the customer's request, and ends when you say good-bye. Remember, telephone customers are going to judge your company by their interactions with you. Ending the call effectively will make them feel good about their choice.

Recap What You Are Going to Do

When you have finished handling the request, assure the customer that you have handled—or will handle—the request. Say something like "Mr. Downs, I've issued a credit for the finance charge." In the case of a lengthy request, it is not necessary to recap each item. You could say "Mr. Downs, I've issued a credit and noted your account of the other item we discussed." If there is a mistake in your recap, the customer will let you know. Doing this will cut down on errors and will ultimately increase customer satisfaction.

Gain the Customer's Agreement

When you recap, the customer knows exactly what you will be doing to handle the request. Wait for an acknowledgment to make sure the customer agrees with your plan. Say something to acknowledge the agreement: "Great. Your order should be shipped out tomorrow."

Ask If You Can Help with Anything Else

Asking if you can help with anything else gives your customer a chance to pause and think before hanging up. If they have forgotten something, they will appreciate the memory jogger. Let the customer know that if he or she needs to call back, you will be happy to help. For example, you might say "My name is Kevin, and if you need to call back I'll be glad to help you." If you work in a large call center that would make it difficult for the customer to reach you personally, you can say "If you need to call back, anyone can access your order, either by the confirmation number or by your name and address."

Thank the Customer for Calling Your Business

Always end on a positive note: "Thank you for calling (name) Company. Have a great day."

PICTURE THIS...
THE RIGHT WAY TO END TELEPHONE CONTACTS

After a short pause, Ashley said "Mrs. Parker, your order for the five items has been processed. Everything is in stock and will be shipped out tomorrow. Do you have a pen and paper handy so I can give you your order number?"

"Yes."

"The number is 061524."

"Okay. Great."

"Is there anything else I can help you with today?"

"No, I think that should do it."

"Again, my name is Ashley. If you need to call back regarding your order, anyone here can reference it by the order number or by your name and address. Thank you for calling VeeJay's, and have a great day."

"Thank you."

How Did the Customer Feel?

Diane was glad that Ashley had recapped the total number of items in her order. And when Ashley asked if she could help with anything else, Diane had the opportunity to think and respond. Diane appreciated that Ashley gave her name and thanked her for calling, and she felt good about contacting this company.

When you call a company as a customer, pay close attention to the way you are treated. Analyze the steps that went well and those that did not. You can learn from thinking about the way you want to be treated as a customer, and then treat your customers in that manner.

PICTURE THIS...
PUTTING IT ALL TOGETHER

"Thank you for calling VeeJay's Sportswear. My name is Ashley. How may I help you today?"

"Hi. I had trouble placing an order online. Can you take the order for me?"

"I'm sorry you had trouble online. I'll be glad to take your order. May I have your name and your billing address?"

"Sure. It's Diane Parker. My address is 23 Sycamore Road. . . ."

"Is that the address where you want your order shipped?"

"Yes."

"It'll take just a minute for my screen to change. How are you doing today?"

"I'm great, how are you?"

"I'm doing well, thank you. Hmm, our system seems to be a little slow this morning, but the screen should come right up." After a short pause, Ashley said "Here we go. I'm ready to take your order now. What is your first catalog number?"

"SU-14236."

"That's the misses' denim jacket. What size and color would you like?"

"Size medium in rose."

"I have the same jacket, and it's really comfortable. What is the next item number?"

"SU-14707."

"Denim slacks. Size and color?"

"Size ten in rose."

"All right. Next?"

Ashley input all the information, adding a personal touch from time to time until Diane finished.

"Thank you. It'll take a moment for the order to process and then I'll give you your order number."

After a short pause, Ashley said "Mrs. Parker, your order for the five items has been processed. Everything is in stock and will be shipped out tomorrow. Do you have a pen and paper handy so I can give you your order number?"

"Yes."

"The number is 061524."

"Okay. Great."

"Is there anything else I can help you with today?"

"No, I think that should do it."

"Again, my name is Ashley. If you need to call back regarding your order, anyone here can reference it by the order number or by your name and address. Thank you for calling VeeJay's, and have a great day."

"Thank you."

The right combination to satisfying customers by telephone is to answer promptly, display a genuine willingness to help, know what to do, do it right, and do it with enthusiasm.

As Your Company's Voice, Always Represent Your Company Well
Competition is greater when you conduct business by phone. Customers have options that extend nationally, even globally in many cases.
Your phone customers may be your primary means of doing business;

BUSINESS
NØT
AS USUAL

but even if they are not, you should always give them the same level of service as your walk-in customers.

What customers want most when they call a business is easy access and hearing a helpful voice. When you answer with enthusiasm and follow through by handling calls effectively and efficiently, you are off to a good start in satisfying your phone customers. If you have an automated system, make it quick, easy, and painless for them and always offer an option to speak to an employee.

Make it your number-one goal to make it easy for your customers to do business with you, and you increase the likelihood that your telephone is going to continue to ring. Always do everything you can to make your phone customers feel welcome, comfortable, and ultimately happy that they called your place of business. Establish your credibility by assuring customers that you can help.

- Your attitude comes through the phone lines; make yours a positive one.

- Smile; your customers will "hear" your smile through your voice.

- Give the customers your full attention.

- Build rapport throughout the contact.

- Always thank your customers for calling the business.

KEY POINTS

Step 1: Welcome Your Customers

- Answer promptly.

- Give the name of your business, your name, and an opening statement or question.

- Listen without interrupting.

- Assure the customer that you can help.

- Work on relationship-building from the beginning of the contact.

Step 2: Find the Best Solutions

- Summarize the customer's opening statement.

- Verbalize what you are doing.

- During pauses, tell the customer what is happening.

- Put your personal touch into the contact.

- Explain why you need to place customers on hold.

Step 3: Show Appreciation

- Recap what you are going to do.

- Gain the customer's agreement.

- Ask if you can help with anything else.

- Thank the customer for calling your business.

P R A C T I C E   L E S S O N

Refer to the customer contact example you wrote down at the beginning of the chapter.

Step 1: Welcome Your Customers

Write down how you will greet your customer.

_____

_____

Step 2: Find the Best Solutions

Summarize the customer's opening statement.

_____

_____

What are some ways you can verbalize what you are doing?

_____

_____

Write down what you might say when there is a pause and what you might say before placing a customer on hold.

_____

_____

Step 3: Show Appreciation

Recap what you are going to do to handle the customer's request.

_____

_____

Write down what you will say to end the contact. (Remember to ask if you can help with anything else and thank the customer for calling your business.)

_____

_____

_____

DOING IT RIGHT!

A while back, I received an email ad for a book manufacturing company. I was unfamiliar with this company, but I occasionally need books printed so I saved the email. Later, when I was working on a manuscript for a client, I reread the email and phoned the company for a job estimate. Rick answered the phone in a professional, helpful manner. After he enthusiastically assured me he could help, I felt I was off to a good start.

Rick completed his paperwork and then emailed me a proposal for my job. Everything looked good—on the surface. I still had doubts, though. I had never done business with this company. It was located far from me, so I had not seen the brick-and-mortar building. Nor had I received a recommendation from a business associate. I hadn't even heard of this company until it sent me that email ad. How could I trust the company when I didn't know anything about it?

That's exactly what I asked Rick. "Everything in your proposal looks great," I said, "but I don't know anything about your company. We haven't established a business relationship. Why should I do business with you when I don't really know who you are and what the outcome is going to be?"

I loved his answer: "We pride ourselves on giving each of our customers the best possible service. We understand it's all about trust. Believe me, I am going to do everything in my power to earn your trust and confidence in me. I will not let you down."

Then he added: "Besides, we're here to stay in business. We know the only way we're going to do that is by giving each customer the best service."

I decided to go with this company because of Rick's confident assurance. I completed the necessary paperwork and trusted him to do the right thing. Surprisingly, he not only did the right thing by producing a good product, he did it sooner than the expected due date, which not only thrilled my client, it more than thrilled me.

I called Rick to thank him and to tell him that he had done exactly what he said he'd do: earn my trust. I pressed him further on how he beat his completion estimate.

Because I'm in the customer-service business, he shared his company's secret. "We have two deadlines: an external one that we give customers, and an internal deadline that we give ourselves. Almost always, we're able to meet our internal deadline, which we know is going to make our customers happy."

Think about that: Here is a small business that figured out a unique way to stand out. When you conduct business by phone, you not only need to earn your customers' trust, you need to do something special to stand out in their minds. That something special is giving outstanding service.

When customers who don't know you are willing to give you their blind trust to do the right thing for them, make it your top priority never to let them down.

H O W   D O   I   M E A S U R E   U P ?

1. What do I do to shut out distractions so that I am able to pay complete attention? What can I do better?

   _____

   _____

2. What do I do to make customers feel welcome and comfortable about calling our company?

   _____

   _____

3. When I am helping customers, do I remember to verbalize what I am doing, especially during pauses and when placing customers on hold? What can I do to improve these telephone skills?

   _____

   _____

4. What do I say to know if each customer is satisfied before ending the call? How can I improve?

   _____

   _____

6

Keeping Up with the Times: Online and Social Media Customer Service

---

**SOCIAL MEDIA IS THE FUTURE OF CUSTOMER SERVICE
AND THE FUTURE IS NOW**

Write down a typical customer contact that is reflective of your online or social media interactions:

_____

_____

_____

_____

_____

Think about the scenario you created as you work through this chapter. Use it as the example when answering the Practice Lesson questions at the end of the chapter.

When the second edition of this book was published, online commerce was becoming an accepted means of conducting business. Fast-forward to today, and it is mind-boggling to realize how quickly we have moved from tiptoeing into shopping and doing business online to witnessing the stampede of the social media era. This opened up another customer service medium: providing customer and support service via social media outlets such as Twitter and Facebook. Customers often prefer the convenience of handling business matters online and through social media rather than driving to a business or wading through lengthy automated answering mazes. Businesses are quickly realizing the value of maintaining not only a website, but also a presence on the social media sites their customers are on.

CUSTOMER SERVICE IS ONLINE AND SOCIAL MEDIA CONTACTS

Consumers have come to rely on the Internet for their business and shopping experiences because it provides convenience and immediacy, both of which people appreciate. Responding quickly to online and social media queries and promptly fulfilling customer requests builds trust and establishes credibility.

As you can imagine, providing online and social media customer service requires yet another skill set. Written communication, your primary means of interacting with online customers, necessitates good writing skills and proper grammar usage. Special care must be taken to make sure that what you write is what you mean to write. Formulating your thoughts clearly and then conveying the correct message is an important skill to develop. Written communication also necessitates the ability to "listen" well. As in listening to an oral conversation, this may well be the most important component of online and social media customer service. When you cannot see or hear the person, your only means of discerning their message is through their written words, so it is vital that you are able to read between the lines, so to speak, to correctly understand the customer's intent.

When you conduct business over the Internet and maintain a social media presence, you open your door to the world. Welcoming your customers into your business begins with maintaining an interesting website and social media presence. Responding quickly to customers' comments, inquiries, and complaints and handling them properly shows that you care about maintaining relationships with them. Following up online to make sure your customers are satisfied with the outcomes of your interactions reflects positively on your professionalism and willingness to satisfy all your customers.

Before we go into online and social media customer service, let's take a moment to focus on your company's presence. While it most likely is not your job to design and maintain your website and social media pages, you know your customers best; therefore, it will be helpful if you understand how your company is portrayed to the public. And since you are your company's chief communicator, it will also be helpful for you to provide feedback to your managers.

BRAINSTORM

As in any customer interaction, you make the best decisions when you know who your online audience is. You learned how to identify your customer base in Chapter 3 by asking: who are your customers, what do they expect from your business, and how do your products and services enhance their lives. Your online audience is your customer base and echoes the answers to these questions.

As a group, review your website and discuss ways in which you can make it more visually appealing and easy to navigate.

■ People tend to prefer a lot of white space on pages when reading computer screens, so keep text to a minimum.

- Photos or other graphics provide interest, as long as they do not slow down the operating speed.

- Make sure the ordering process is easy by monitoring the product-information page, shopping cart, customer registration, billing information, and final checkout.

- If appropriate, include warranty or guarantee information and information about technical support on your site, as that may increase customer trust.

- Customers may learn about your company through a search engine, so select words and phrases for your title pages they are likely to use for keyword searches.

- Include a "contact" button for easy emailing.

- Link your website to your social media accounts.

- Designate employees to monitor and reply to email requests.

- If you offer live chat, respond quickly, handle requests correctly, and make sure the customer is satisfied before ending the chat.

As a group, review your social media pages and discuss ways in which you can make them more visually appealing to customers.

- Choose attractive and relevant content.

- Post pictures to build brand awareness, such as your company logo, products, or your support staff.

- Post regular updates. Change pictures, share tips, showcase new products, or add photos of the customer-service staff in action.

- Advertise specials, sales, or anything out of the ordinary.

- Include status updates for announcements.

- Offer your customers and potential customers something for free, such as providing tips, a link to your newsletter or blog, or contests and giveaways.

- Ask for customer feedback.

- When a customer publicly posts a complaint, respond with an assurance that you want to resolve the issue and ask the customer to message the details. Then take the issue off-line.

- Designate staff to monitor and respond to customers.

- Provide the same level of service as you would for in-person or telephone customers.

If you are new to this arena, Facebook and Twitter may be your first choices for your social media presence, since those are currently two of the most utilized social media networks for businesses. Other sites such as Pinterest, Instagram, YouTube, and Tumblr may also prove to be advantageous to you. It will be most helpful for you to find out where your audience is and establish a presence. New sites are being created continuously, so it is essential to keep up to date on which ones are pertinent to your business. In addition, sites created specifically for customer reviews can help consumers make purchasing decisions. Some popular ones are Yelp, TripAdvisor, Angie's List, and the Better Business Bureau. It is in every company's best interest to manage review sites that are germane to their industry. Remember that while it may not be your job to establish a presence on these sites, it will be helpful to your company if you provide feedback on what you feel may be significant to your customers.

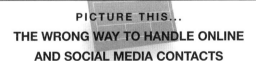

PICTURE THIS...
THE WRONG WAY TO HANDLE ONLINE
AND SOCIAL MEDIA CONTACTS

Ethan was hired for his first full-time job after graduating from college. Realizing that his wardrobe needed updating, he searched online and found a company that carried a brand of clothes he liked. He placed his order and, because he needed the items quickly, he upgraded the shipping option to two days, which would get the order to him by Wednesday, in plenty of time for his first day on Monday.

Wednesday morning Ethan checked the tracking, which showed delivery for the following Tuesday. He called the company and explained the situation. The employee apologized, explained that the expedited option had been overlooked, and unfortunately the order would not be delivered until Tuesday. There was nothing she could do because it had already been shipped, although she would credit the shipping rate back to the regular rate.

Ethan hung up, furious because he felt the employee did not understand the urgency of his situation. He felt that she could have offered to place a new order and ship it overnight. If that was not possible, at the very least she could have shown more empathy and credited the shipping to no charge. And she could have offered a discount coupon for a future order. He wrote a displeased comment on Twitter. *@xyzcompany Worst customer service. Paid for 2-day shipping, did not happen. Employee did nothing to help.*

He was not surprised when the company failed to respond.

What Went Wrong?

The employee apologized but did not offer any resolution other than to reduce the shipping rate. When he posted a negative comment on Twitter and the company failed to respond, Ethan vowed never to order from the company again.

How Did the Customer Feel?

Ethan had every right to be upset, especially because his perception was that the employee did not understand the urgency of the situation. He needed the clothes before Monday. He felt she could have done something more than just reduce the shipping charge. Ethan was so angered by the employee's uncaring attitude that he posted a Twitter complaint, which made him even angrier when the company did not respond.

When you conduct online business, you open your door to customers around the globe. Consider that customers who transact business online put their blind faith in your company. When potential customers view your website, they have no idea what your brick-and-mortar business looks like. They have no idea if you even have a traditional brick-and-mortar business. They cannot tell if your company is a multimillion-dollar corporation, a small business run out of a strip-mall location, or a one-person operation based at home. Valuing your online customers and giving them exceptional service can develop into long-term relationships. Customers who interact with a business online deserve the same level of service as face-to-face and telephone customers. It does not matter how large or small your company is; what does matter is that you handle your online customers with professionalism and courtesy. Master the following steps and you will be able to handle these interactions successfully.

Step 1: Welcome Your Customers

Step 2: Find the Best Solutions

Step 3: Show Appreciation

In Ethan's situation, the employee could have offered some sort of compensation other than merely reducing the shipping rate. When Ethan posted a complaint on Twitter, the company should have responded and made restitution. Mistakes can happen. It is what a company does afterward that can make or break a relationship.

STEP 1
WELCOME YOUR CUSTOMERS

Welcoming your online customers into your business should be handled in the same manner in which you welcome in-person and telephone customers. Understanding what online customers expect will help you welcome them in. Inviting your potential customers to do business with you begins on your home page and social media accounts by providing pertinent information that is easy to read, easy to comprehend, and visually appealing. Welcoming customers by responding quickly to requests is essential if you want to satisfy online customers. And maintaining an updated, ongoing presence will keep your customers and potential customers interested in what you have to offer.

Understand What Online Customers Expect

Customers want to know you are legitimate. You can demonstrate that by letting your visitors know that you stand behind your products by posting your product and service guarantees. Customers also want to know you are trustworthy. You can demonstrate that by promptly replying to email, social media, and live-chat queries, by processing requests quickly, and by following up to ensure satisfaction.

Invite Customers in to Your Business

When you open up your business to online customers, you do not know when they "come in" to your business. You do not have the option to smile and offer a friendly greeting. You do not have the option to speak in an upbeat, helpful tone of voice. So how do you invite customers in to your business? Review the tips in the brainstorm sidebar. Your website and social media home pages can invite customers in by being visually interesting through their pictures, graphics, and written content, and by offering customers a reason to want to "come in." Update your pages frequently and include information that will interest your audience enough to make them want to do business with you.

Respond Quickly and Appropriately

You build credibility and establish trust by being responsive to both existing and potential customers. Give your online customers the same consideration as if they were there in person or speaking to you by telephone. When your means of interacting with customers is through the written word, remember to use the same words you would use if you were speaking directly to the person. Thank customers for their interest in your company and products. Anticipate questions they may have and address them in your emails and social media posts. Choose uplifting, constructive words. When a customer is upset, choose compassionate, caring words. Remember to use proper grammar and courteous words and phrases.

When someone posts a compliment on your Facebook page, reply with a positive comment: *Thank you! We're so glad you enjoyed your dinner last night.* When someone asks a question, posting the answer online may answer the question for others: *Thanks for asking about our turnaround time. We always strive to ship orders by the next business day.* When some-one complains online, assure the customer that you are going to help: *I'm sorry you had trouble ordering the baseball bat. Please message me with details & contact number. I'll check & call you back.*

Maintain an Ongoing Presence

When you continually post new information, you keep your customers and potential customers interested. Think of ways in which your company can continually update its online accounts. Reach out to your audience and make it enjoyable for visitors to want to stay connected with your company.

PICTURE THIS...
THE RIGHT WAY TO WELCOME ONLINE
AND SOCIAL MEDIA CONTACTS

Ethan was hired for his first full-time job after graduating from college. Realizing that his wardrobe needed updating, he searched online and found a company that carried a brand of clothes he liked. He placed his order and, because he needed the items quickly, he upgraded the shipping option to two days, which would get the order to him by Wednesday, in plenty of time for his first day on Monday.

Wednesday morning, Ethan checked the tracking, which showed delivery for the following Tuesday. He called the company and explained the situation. The employee apologized and explained that the expedited option had been overlooked and the order would be delivered Tuesday. There was nothing she could do, although she would credit the shipping rate back to the regular rate.

Ethan hung up, furious because he felt the employee did not under-stand the urgency of his situation. He was so upset that he wrote a displeased comment on Twitter. *@xyzcompany Worst customer service. Paid for 2-day shipping, did not happen. Employee did nothing to help.*

He was not expecting a reply and was pleasantly surprised when he received the following response: *I am sorry this happened. Please DM me with the details of your order & your contact number. I will look into this immediately.*

How Did the Customer Feel?

Even though Ethan felt the person with whom he had spoken by telephone could have handled the problem better, he hoped the employee who responded to his Twitter complaint might be able to do something.

STEP 2
FIND THE BEST SOLUTIONS

The most important aspect for customers who connect with a company through email, live-chat, or social media channels is that they want to know they are interacting with a person who has understanding, compassion, enthusiasm, and concern: a real person with real feelings who will take care of their requests. Learning how to listen to what you are reading is possible when you learn to read every word and read without your own emotions or biases. Taking care of the issue in the same manner you would handle an in-person or telephone customer will build a trusting relationship. Being able to write as you would voice a message, and then reading your message before posting or hitting the SEND button will help you communicate the right message to customers. Finally, projecting soft skills shows that you are a real person with a real voice who understands and relates to your customers.

Listen Carefully

People may write in a way that makes it difficult for you to understand the message when you first read it. Someone for whom English is not the first language may write in a way that impedes your ability to decipher the message correctly. You may also read with preconceived biases, read judgmentally, or jump to conclusions before finishing the entire message.

When reading any message, it will be helpful to read word for word and keep your emotions out of it. Read the entire message before deciding on your course of action. If you are unsure, read the message a second time. If you are still unsure, ask for a clarification. For example: *Thank you for your inquiry. I want to make sure I understand correctly that you would like to know the cost for shipping twenty gadgets.* Now the customer can confirm or clarify before you proceed.

Handle the Issue Quickly and Correctly

When customers do business online, they want to know that their requests will be handled right away. Customers appreciate efficiency and effectiveness; handle all requests in the same manner you handle your face-to-face and telephone customers. When communicating through writing, tell your customer exactly what you have done or will do to take care of the request and when it will be completed. Think of what information your customer needs to know and answer the questions: who (will take care of it), what (will be done), when (will it be done), where (if applicable), and how (if applicable). *Ms. Elliott, thank you for taking the time to contact us about your bill. I apologize that you were incorrectly charged for a second service call. I have credited the $15.00, which will be reflected on your next bill.*

Write Carefully

Effective communication is the same whether you speak or write your message. Customers will find it easier to understand when you get in the habit of using correct grammar and courtesy words and phrases every time you speak and write. Remember to avoid the use of jargon, company terms, and slang, because your customers are not likely to understand them.

When responding to email, social media, or live-chat queries, interject the same phrases of assurance and appreciation that you would use when verbally communicating with a customer: *I'll be happy to take care of your billing inquiry;* or *Yes, we have that in stock and can ship it to you today;* or *I've placed the order for you: The order number is _____.* Keep your messages short and to the point. When customers see a long block of text, chances are they are going to skip over parts of the message.

We live in a world made up of many cultures, customs, and languages. Even though we may appear to be different from each other, many communication skills are universal. Basic courtesies, respect, willingness to help, compassion, and a positive attitude communicate worldwide, even without being able to understand a particular language. When writing to a person from another culture, write in your words rather than trying to mimic their manner of writing. Write in your normal voice and always be professional in your responses.

Always treat other people as you want to be treated. Did you know there is a version of the Golden Rule in every culture? The words, depending on the origin, are different from those you may have learned, but the meaning is the same in every culture. When you treat others with respect, consideration, courtesy, compassion, and kindness, you will be able to effectively work through any language, cultural, or other barriers.

Show Your Soft Side

Your online and social customers are like any other customers. When people send a written message, they want to know they are dealing with a human being. Always put your personal touch in your writing and project your personality in your replies. Picture yourself as communicating with a customer who is in your business. Let your personality come through in your written messages by being responsive, friendly, and professional at all times. It helps to write as you would say it. If you are unsure of your wording, read the message out loud to hear how it sounds. Does it sound the same as though you were speaking the words?

Work on relationship building with your online customers by thanking them for their interest in your company. Use your social media networks effectively by continually posting helpful information about sales, discounts, or new products. Send emails to your repeat customers to let them know about upcoming events and updates about your company.

Keeping your company's name in customers' minds can result in loyalty, and it tells all your customers that you value their business.

If you are not accessible 24/7, let your audience know when you are open. If you are closed weekends, specify this on your website and social media pages so those who contact you on Friday evening will not look for a reply throughout the weekend.

PICTURE THIS...
THE RIGHT WAY TO HANDLE CUSTOMER
REQUESTS BY FINDING THE BEST SOLUTIONS

Ethan wrote the following direct message: *re: order number 1384572. I am starting a new job next Monday and needed new work clothes. I placed an order on Monday and opted for two-day delivery. I expected the order to be delivered on Wednesday. When I checked the tracking info, it showed delivery for next Tuesday. I called the 800 number and the employee I spoke to told me that unfortunately the expedited shipping had been overlooked and the order was shipped normal with a delivery for next Tuesday. She said she would adjust the shipping charge back to the regular rate. I told her that Tuesday is too late and she should just cancel the order. She said she couldn't do that. This situation is unacceptable. I need the items before I start my new job. Now I have to go out looking for new work clothes when I expected to receive them from a company I have always liked.* He reread his message and sent it.

Within thirty minutes, he received the following reply: *My name is Melissa and I am going to take care of this for you. I apologize that your order was not shipped to arrive by Wednesday. I completely understand how frustrating this has been since you are starting a new job and need these items. Here is what I can do for you: I can reorder the items to be shipped overnight and I will waive the shipping charge. I can reroute the order that has already been shipped back to us and credit you for that order. If this is satisfactory, please reply so that we have adequate time to fulfill the order and get the order shipped out today. Again, please accept my apology on behalf of our company.*

Ethan responded with a huge thank-you and confirmation that he would like the order shipped overnight.

How Did the Customer Feel?

Ethan not only appreciated the quick response, he appreciated Melissa's thoughtful and personal response in understanding how important this order was since he was starting a new job. It no longer mattered that the telephone employee had not given him a satisfactory resolution. He was happy that his Twitter complaint was read, an employee responded, assured him she was going to help, and told him exactly what she could do. Ethan felt confident that Melissa would rectify the situation satisfactorily.

STEP 3
SHOW APPRECIATION

Ending a written interaction is the same as saying goodbye to a face-to-face or telephone customer. Recap what you have done—or will do—to handle the query. Make sure the customer agrees with your course of action. Find out if you can help with anything else. Thank the customer. It's that simple. And you have an advantage. Because you are writing rather than speaking, you have backspace and delete keys. You have the ability to read and revise before sending. You have the ability to end your written interactions in a manner that leaves your customers satisfied.

Explain What Actions You Are Taking

When you take the time to recap, your customers know exactly what you have done or plan to do. This gives customers the opportunity to tell you if you understand their requests correctly. For example, you write *Mrs. Hall, I will note your account that you are returning the thingamabob. We will credit your credit card as soon as we receive it.*

Give the Customer a Chance to Agree or Disagree

By taking the time to recap your actions, the customer will let you know if she agrees or not. Mrs. Hall may either reply: *Excellent. Thank you.* or *No, I'm not returning it. I want to exchange it for a silver one.* Now you know how to reply. *My mistake. I will note your account that you want to exchange the copper thingamabob for one in silver. As soon as we receive it, we will send out a silver one to you.* Wait for the customer's acknowledgement before proceeding. *Yes, that's right. I'll send the copper one back today in exchange for the silver.* Now it is your turn to acknowledge the agreement. *Great. I've noted your account.* It is always better to be a little wordy rather than act on assumptions.

Always Ask if You Can Help with Anything Else

This is a common courtesy. It gives the customer the opportunity to think if he needs to ask you something else. *Yes, thanks for asking. I almost forgot. I'd like to request a catalog.* You respond: *I've ordered our new Fall catalog sent to you. You should receive it within a week.* Offer a closing statement. *My name is Connor. Please don't hesitate to contact me if you have any other questions.*

End the Contact on a Positive Note

Write something to show that you appreciate the customer. *I'm glad I was able to assist you, and I hope you have a wonderful rest of your day.* Not only does this add a personal touch, it reflects positively on your company as well.

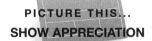

PICTURE THIS...
SHOW APPRECIATION

Melissa explained what actions she was going to take. *I will reorder the five items to be shipped overnight and billed to the credit card on file. I am waiving the shipping charge. I rerouted the existing order back to our warehouse and credited your account for that order in the amount of*

$257.34. I will message you with the UPS tracking number shortly.

Because he knew exactly what she planned to do, Ethan had the opportunity to agree or clear up any misunderstandings. *Yes, that's great. Thank you!*

Melissa acknowledged his agreement. *You're welcome. Is there anything else I can do for you today?*

Ethan was more than pleased. *I appreciate all your help and I look forward to receiving my order tomorrow.*

Melissa ended the interaction. *I'm so glad I was able to help. I will send you the tracking number shortly and I will follow up to make sure your order arrives tomorrow. Have a terrific afternoon.*

The next day, Melissa sent another direct message. *Hi, Ethan. I just checked and saw that we delivered your order. Best of luck in your new job!*

How Did the Customer Feel?

Because she took the time to recap her proposed actions, Ethan knew exactly what she was going to do. Melissa communicated effectively throughout this contact and gave him the opportunity to agree before she proceeded. Ethan appreciated that she asked if she could do anything else, and he was pleasantly surprised that she took the time the following day to wish him luck in his new job.

Whether you are responding via email, a social media post, or live-chat, the right combination to satisfying your online customers is by demonstrating that you are trustworthy; by being accessible; by responding quickly; and by communicating effectively with your online customers.

PICTURE THIS...
PUTTING IT ALL TOGETHER

Ethan was hired for his first full-time job after graduating from college. Realizing that his wardrobe needed updating, he searched online and found a company that carried a brand of clothes he liked. He placed his order and, because he needed the items quickly, he upgraded the shipping option to two days, which would get the order to him by Wednesday, in plenty of time for his first day on Monday.

Wednesday morning, Ethan checked the tracking, which showed delivery for the following Tuesday. He called the company and explained the situation. The employee apologized and explained that the expedited option had been overlooked and the order would be delivered Tuesday. There was nothing she could do, although she would credit the shipping rate back to the regular rate.

Ethan hung up, furious because he felt the employee did not understand the urgency of his situation. He was so upset that he wrote a displeased comment on Twitter. *@xyzcompany Worst customer service. Paid for 2-day shipping. Did not happen. Employee did nothing to help.* He was not expecting a reply and was pleasantly surprised when he received the following reply: *I am sorry this happened. Please DM me with the details of your order & your contact number. I will look into this immediately.*

Ethan wrote the following direct message: *re: order number 1384572. I am starting a new job next Monday and needed new work clothes. I placed an order on Monday and opted for two-day delivery. I expected the order to be delivered on Wednesday. When I checked the tracking info, it showed delivery for next Tuesday. I called the 800 number and the employee I spoke to told me that unfortunately the expedited shipping had been overlooked and the order was shipped regular with a delivery for next Tuesday. She said she would adjust the shipping charge back to the regular rate. I told her that Tuesday is too late and she should just cancel the order. She said she couldn't do that. This situation is unacceptable. I need the items before I start my new job. Now I have to go out looking for new work clothes when I expected to receive them from a company I have always liked.* He reread his message and sent it.

Within thirty minutes, he received the following reply: *My name is Melissa and I am going to take care of this for you. I apologize that your order was not shipped to arrive by Wednesday. I completely understand how frustrating this has been since you are starting a new job and need these items. Here is what I can do for you: I can reorder the items to be shipped overnight, and I will waive the shipping charge. I can reroute the order that has already been shipped back to us and credit you for that order. If this is satisfactory, please reply so that we have adequate time to fulfill the order and get the order shipped out today. Again, please accept my apology on behalf of our company.*

Ethan responded with a huge thank-you and confirmation that he would like the order shipped overnight.

Melissa explained what actions she was going to take. *I will reorder the five items to be shipped overnight and billed to the credit card on file. I am waiving the shipping charge. I rerouted the existing order back to our warehouse and credited your account for that order in the amount of $257.34. I will message you with the UPS tracking number shortly.*

Because he knew exactly what she planned to do, Ethan had the opportunity to agree or clear up any misunderstandings. *Yes, that's great. Thank you!*

Melissa acknowledged his agreement. *You're welcome. Is there anything else I can do for you today?*

Ethan was more than pleased. *I appreciate all your help and I look forward to receiving my order tomorrow.*

Melissa ended the interaction. *I'm so glad I was able to help. I will send you the tracking number shortly, and I will follow up to make sure your order arrives tomorrow. Have a terrific afternoon.*

The next day Melissa sent another direct message. *Hi Ethan. I just checked and saw that we delivered your order. Best of luck in your new job!*

Social Media Is the Future of Customer Service, and the Future Is Now

Many experts believe that social media truly is the future of customer service. Keep in mind that no matter the venue for customer contact, customers will always want to know they are communicating with a person. When you interact through the written word, you have the benefit of making sure that you write exactly what you mean to write. You also have the opportunity to add a personal touch to your writing.

When you make the commitment to communicate with your customers through email, social media posts, or live-chat, you can develop a loyal customer base by giving your online customers the same level of service you give to your local customers.

Welcoming your customers by offering an easy-to-navigate website or social media page, responding quickly to queries, and handling requests expeditiously keep the conversation in real time and will increase your chance of online success. Frequently updating your site pages will keep your customers interested in your company. Welcoming every opportunity to build your business will help you keep pace with ever-changing technology.

- Continually look for new social media sites that are of interest to your customers.

- Demonstrate to your online customers that you are trustworthy and credible by handling requests quickly and correctly.

- Go the extra mile for your online customers by following up to make sure they are satisfied with the outcome of your conversation.

- Remember that each of your customers is the reason you have a job, whether you can see them or not.

KEY POINTS

Step 1: Welcome Your Customers

- Understand what online customers expect.

- Invite customers in to your business.

- Respond quickly and appropriately.

- Maintain an ongoing presence.

Step 2: Find the Best Solutions

- Listen carefully.

- Handle the issue quickly and correctly.

- Write carefully.

- Show your soft side.

Step 3: Show Appreciation

- Explain what actions you are taking.

- Give the customer a chance to agree or disagree.

- Always ask if you can help with anything else.

- End the contact on a positive note.

P R A C T I C E   L E S S O N

Refer to the customer contact example you wrote down at the beginning of the chapter.

Step 1: Welcome Your Customers

Write down your opening statement.

_____

_____

Step 2: Find the Best Solutions

Write a sentence to explain your proposed solution. Include a statement to show your soft side.

_____

_____

Step 3: Show Appreciation

Assuming the customer has agreed, write a closing.

_____

_____

D O I N G   I T   R I G H T !

Promoting products and services on popular sites such as Facebook and Twitter has provided companies with another outlet to reach customers and potential customers. Donsuemor Bakery, based in Alameda, California, is an example of a company that has mastered social media. While visiting my family in California, I stumbled upon the bakery's prepackaged madeleines in a coffee shop. From the first bite, I was hooked. When I returned home, I visited the website and was disappointed to read that the products aren't available in stores on the East Coast where I live. The website was visually appealing, the product pages were clear and informative, and the order process was easy. Since placing that first online order, I have become a huge fan of Donsuemor baked goods.

When I saw the social media links on the Donsuemor website, I began following the bakery on Facebook. To say that it has mastered the art of promotion and communication through social media is really an understatement. The bakery posts a daily update. It might be a recipe idea for one of the products, a video clip of an employee, an announcement of a new product, a description of a product, an advertisement about where to purchase, a request for customer input, or . . . I could go on and on about the interesting daily posts that always include a mouthwatering picture. My personal favorite is the random "giveaway Friday" drawings. *Tell us what you like most about ___ for a chance to win a box of ___.* I look forward to looking at the daily pictures and reading the posts. I really get excited when it's a giveaway day! I even won one time.

The most important key to using social media effectively is not to bombard your audience with useless information. Post applicable, interesting, and timely information. This is what Donsuemor does best. The bakery posts once a day, and the posts are always noteworthy. Baked goods eye candy!

What I appreciate most is that someone at Donsuemor regularly monitors and responds to customers. Post a compliment and an employee is likely to offer a heartfelt thank-you. When the company asks for customer feedback on a product, it responds to customers' input. I've never read an online complaint about Donsuemor, but I would be willing to say without a doubt it will respond to and rectify any problem.

Here is a company that I regularly do business with, yet I have never been to the store. I don't even know where Alameda, California is. I saw the madeleines in a coffee shop and decided to try them. Of course, the first step in building a successful business is to offer great products. The madeleines are that and more. Since I began following the bakery on Facebook, I am reminded daily how much I love its products. When Donsuemor announces a new product, I usually go right to their website to see if I can order online.

If your company hasn't yet established a social media presence, why wait? Find out which networks your audience is likely to visit. Set up an account. Ask your employees for input. Learn from other companies that have figured out how to successfully market on social media. Then figure out the best ways to promote your products and services. Always monitor and respond. At first it may be trial and error, but for the long term it sure can't hurt.

H O W   D O   I   M E A S U R E   U P ?

1. How well do we create a vision of our company on our social media sites?

   _____

   _____

   _____

   _____

2. Do we regularly post information that will be helpful and interesting to our customers? What are some things we can do that we aren't doing?

_____

_____

_____

_____

3.   How accessible are we to our social-media customers? Do we
     respond quickly and process requests promptly? What can we do to
     improve?

_____

_____

_____

_____

CHAPTER

Giving When Getting Is Not Expected: Self-Service Contacts

ALWAYS GIVE CUSTOMERS MORE THAN THEY EXPECT,

EVEN WHEN THEY DO IT THEMSELVES

Write down a typical customer contact that is reflective of your self-service interactions:

_____

_____

_____

_____

_____

_____

Think about this scenario as you work through this chapter. Use it as the example when answering the Practice Lesson questions at the end of the chapter.

Customers encounter self-service operations in dealing with many businesses. You can use self-checkout stations to pay for your purchases at most grocery, big-box discount, and home-improvement stores. You can withdraw money from your bank account on ATM machines. You can purchase gasoline with a swipe of your credit card. You can book airline tickets and check in online. You can check in and check out of hotels using on-site kiosks. And probably the most widely used self-service offerings are found on websites, where you can place and track orders, review your accounts, and pay bills online. Simply stated, consumers like the ability to speed up transactions by doing it themselves.

Self-service has made it easy for consumers to do business . . . when all goes well. The upsides of self-service are that it is convenient, quick, efficient, and offers increased control over how you conduct your business. However, the operative words are "when all goes well." The downsides of self-service are that there is a learning curve, assistance is not always available if there is a problem, and the wait time may be longer than expected if someone ahead of you is confused or slow and backs up other customers. An additional downside for some customers is that they do not welcome self-service options and prefer interacting with a real person.

CUSTOMER SERVICE IS SELF-SERVICE CONTACTS

Offering basic courtesies, communicating well, and building relationships can be accomplished even when customers serve themselves. Most consumers have become comfortable with self-service and appreciate its convenience, although they may not have high service expectations since they are completing their transactions without the help of an employee. Self-service should never mean no-service! Customers want to know an employee is available to help them, if needed. When things go wrong, customers do expect someone to handle problems right away; and if no one is available, they may quickly become frustrated. When you find ways to provide service in self-service settings, you will stand out in your customers' minds in a positive way.

In-store settings offer a great opportunity to give your customers more than they expect. When you are actively involved in observing and moving the flow along, you show your customers that you are interested in them, that you appreciate their business. If your business primarily handles phone or Internet contacts, you can still give customers more than they expect by providing clear instructions as to how these customers may reach an employee. Whether your self-service offerings are primarily in-store, phone, or Internet-based, you have a valuable opportunity to greet customers, to assist with transactions by looking for opportunities to help, and to end interactions on a positive note by making sure customers are satisfied and by thanking them for choosing to do business with you. Leaving a positive lasting impression stays with customers long after they finish their transaction. When you offer self-service options, your customers will appreciate the convenience—as long as you make the interaction convenient for them.

BRAINSTORM

Think about a recent self-service interaction in which you were the customer. What was your reaction to your contact with the business after serving yourself?

- *What did the business do that made you feel comfortable?*

- *Was help readily available?*

- *When you completed your transaction, did the employee (or message on the automated phone system or website screen) say something that made you feel valued?*

Now, think about your business. Walk through a self-service contact, viewing it as though you are experiencing it for the first time. Then answer the questions above from a customer's standpoint.

Remember to pay close attention to all details—your customers will. Find ways to improve your self-service interactions. Review this process frequently to make sure that you always give your customers, both self-service and traditional, more than they expect.

PICTURE THIS...
THE WRONG WAY TO HANDLE SELF-SERVICE INTERACTIONS

Tina stopped by the grocery store to pick up the items she needed to make dinner. This was part of her usual routine on her way home from work, and she usually did it with little thought: She'd run in, grab a basket, find the items on her list, and then find the shortest checkout line.

Today was different, though. For some reason, every checkout counter had at least two people waiting in line with full carts. She noticed that one of the self-check registers was available. She preferred letting a cashier check her out but decided to use self-serve after noticing a cashier standing at a podium in the self-check area.

Tina scanned the bar code on her first item and placed it in the bag. When she placed the second item in the bag, she heard a recorded voice saying, "Place the item in the bag." *It is in the bag,* she thought. The voice sounded again. "Place the item in the bag." Embarrassed, she lifted the item and put it back in the bag, which stopped the recording.

Noticing another customer waiting to use the self-checkout, Tina hurriedly picked up the next item in her basket, a bunch of broccoli. There was no bar code to scan. She read the screen and touched the button for produce. The screen prompted her to enter the four-digit number. *What four-digit number?* When Tina could not find a four-digit number on the broccoli, she looked to the podium where the employee had been standing, but he was gone.

Now she noticed that two customers were waiting behind her. Tina felt frustrated that no employee was there to help her. She gathered up her items and left the self-checkout area. When she saw that the regular checkout lines were still long, she made a quick decision: *I think we'll order takeout tonight.* She quickly put her items back and left the grocery store without making a purchase.

What Went Wrong?

Let's begin by noting what went right. Tina made the decision to try the self-checkout lanes because she noticed that an employee appeared to be available for assistance. Had that employee been paying attention when

Tina was checking out, he would have seen that she did not know where to find the code for the broccoli. This would have been a great training moment for the employee to show her how to find the list of codes. Because Tina became frustrated when no one was available to help, the experience left a negative impression.

How Did the Customer Feel?

When Tina noticed that someone was waiting behind her, she felt uncomfortable because she was having trouble. She became frustrated while trying to check out without any assistance and walked away in the middle of her transaction, opting not to buy groceries at all.

When you offer self-service to your customers, you offer them control over the way they do business with you. The most important thing to remember is that you can find ways to provide great service in self-service situations. Always look for ways to help your customers, even those who are comfortable helping themselves, by being friendly and approachable.

Learn the following, and you will provide exceptional service to your self-service customers:

Step 1: Welcome Your Customers

Step 2: Find the Best Solutions

Step 3: Show Appreciation

Tina's poor first impression of self-checkout was her last impression of self-checkout. Had the employee taken the time to ease her discomfort by providing help when she needed it, Tina would have gained confidence to try it the next time she shopped.

STEP 1
WELCOME YOUR CUSTOMERS

The most important thing you can do to welcome self-serve customers is to make it easy for them to use the self-serve options. Greeting your customers with a welcoming statement either in person, on the phone, or on your home page will put any customer at ease, even those using a self-service option for the first time. When customers are willing to serve themselves, they still want to know that an employee is available if they need help.

Make It Easy

The only way you will know if you are making it easy for your self-serve customers is to know your customers. Know who they are and what they expect. Baby boomers, who are used to interacting with employees to take care of their needs, will have a different expectation about self-serve than millennials, who grew up comfortably using technology. If you are not sure what your customers want, ask them. While asking for customer input on your processes may not officially be your job, it is your job to gauge customers' satisfaction. As your company's interface, you know best if your self-serve options are meeting their needs. And the key here is meeting *their* needs, not your company's. Try walking through a typical transaction. How easy is it to do business with you? If you find room for improvement, give feedback to your manager.

Greet Every Customer

Offering a warm greeting to your self-service customers will help you begin to make a great first impression with them. In in-store settings, smile, make eye contact, say hello, and give the customer your name. If your company uses automated phone answering, include in your greeting a path to reach a live person by offering an extension number or a dial-zero option. For Internet interactions, state on your home page how to reach a person. This can be done by providing an 800 number, an email button, or a live-chat option.

Be Ready to Help

This is the most important goal of accustoming your customers to using your self-service processes. There is always a learning curve associated with moving into a new practice. Just as you need time to teach or learn new company procedures, policies, and products, your customers need time to learn and feel comfortable using self-service. Tell the customer you are available to help. If it is your job to work in the self-serve area, always make sure you are available and be observant of customers who need assistance.

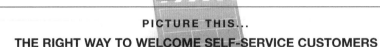

PICTURE THIS...

THE RIGHT WAY TO WELCOME SELF-SERVICE CUSTOMERS

Tina stopped by the grocery store to pick up the items she needed to make dinner. This was part of her usual routine on her way home from work, and she usually did it with little thought: She'd run in, grab a basket, find the items on her list, and then find the shortest checkout line.

Today was different, though. For some reason, every checkout line had at least two people waiting with full carts. She looked over to the self-checkout area and noticed that one of the cash registers was available. She preferred letting a cashier check her out but decided to use self-serve after noticing a cashier standing at a podium in the self-check area.

Tina set her basket down on the shelf and the cashier at the podium said "Hi, my name is Ted. I'll be right here if you need any help."

"Thank you," Tina replied.

How Did the Customer Feel?

Tina preferred using the traditional checkout lane with a cashier because she liked the employee interaction. When Ted smiled, made eye contact, and greeted her warmly, she felt comfortable knowing that help was available. She began forming a positive first impression.

STEP 2
FIND THE BEST SOLUTIONS

Most customers who choose self-service are not going to need your help. However, problems may occur and a problem can fluster even the most experienced user. In in-store situations, the price may not scan, the customer may have a coupon you need to process, or the screen may be stuck. In Internet situations, there might be a computer glitch, the screen may freeze, or the customer may not be able to locate the correct choice. In phone situations, the automated system is not going to be the best outcome for every contact. Customers may have a question not covered by the selections offered, or they may need to discuss something with an employee. When you pay attention to customers needing help and step in before frustration sets in, your customers will feel valued.

Monitor the Flow

This is easiest to do in in-store settings, because you can spot customers who are inexperienced or having a problem. By observing the flow of self-service cash registers and kiosks, you will be in a position to step in and help when needed. By watching for long lines, you will be able to find out why bottlenecks are occurring and do what you need to do to move the process along. In phone and Internet interactions you are not going to know when your customers need help. In these situations, offering a way to reach an employee is the best alternative you can provide to increase your customer's comfort level when they serve themselves. When you speak to a customer who is likely to be frustrated, show empathy and willingness to complete the interaction.

Look for Teaching Moments

Again, this is easiest when you are face to face with your customers. Be on the lookout for ways to teach customers how to best use your self-service equipment. Step in before customers become so frustrated that, like Tina, they leave the area and perhaps even your place of business. The path of least resistance will be for you to take over for your customers; however, when you do this your customers are not learning and they may encounter the same problem in the future. Rather, offer to train them: "This can be confusing when you aren't used to it. I'll be happy to show you how to do it." Show and tell your customers, but allow them to complete the transaction by moving through screens and entering their own information.

For phone and Internet interactions, your teaching moments are likely to come after a customer reaches you to tell you about a problem. Take the time to walk each customer through the transaction. If you feel it best to alleviate customer frustration, offer to handle the request, explaining the steps as you proceed. If you encounter the same complaint repeatedly, let your manager know so that it can be remedied.

Make Your Self-Service Customers Feel Valued

Whether you provide service in traditional settings or through self-service, you can find ways to make your customers feel valued. In self-service situations, the best way to do this is by communicating to your customers that you are happy to help, and then by looking for ways to do so. When customers feel valued, you are building a positive relationship and they will be more likely to use your business's self-service options again.

TIP

If you work in a retail store and are assigned to the self-service checkout area, try getting out from behind your workstation. From time to time, walk around or stand in the center of the area. Customers will see you as approachable, friendly, and willing to help.

PICTURE THIS...
THE RIGHT WAY TO HANDLE SELF-SERVICE CUSTOMER REQUESTS

Tina scanned the bar code on her first item and placed it in the bag. When she placed the second item in the bag, she heard a recorded voice saying "Place the item in the bag." *It is in the bag,* she thought. The voice sounded again: "Place the item in the bag." "I don't know why that happens," Ted said as he walked over to Tina. "Sometimes the weight isn't picked up. Try picking up the can and putting it back in the bag."

Tina did as Ted suggested, and the voice stopped. Feeling a little embarrassed, she smiled at Ted. He noticed that someone was waiting to check out, so he backed up but stayed in the center of the checkout area.

Tina hurriedly picked up the next item in her basket, a bunch of broccoli. When she placed her broccoli on the scanner and looked confused, Ted walked back over to her. "The screen is going to prompt you to enter a four-digit number. If you can't find it on the produce, the items are listed on this roller." Ted pointed above the screen and showed Tina how to find broccoli.

"Thank you so much for helping me." Tina scanned the rest of her items.

How Did the Customer Feel?

Because Ted stepped in to help, Tina felt comfortable learning how to use the self-check. She appreciated that he had noticed that she needed help and came to her assistance before she asked for it. She also appreciated that he had taken the time to train her.

STEP 3
SHOW APPRECIATION

When you take the time to properly end self-service contacts, you go a long way to making your customers feel that they matter to you. Being attentive, making sure customers are satisfied, and saying something to show that you value their business will leave a positive lasting impression.

Pay Attention

Again, this is easiest when a customer is face to face. Take a moment to monitor customers' facial expressions as they complete their transactions. Paying attention to nonverbal cues will give you a good idea of their level of satisfaction. If you think someone is displeased, ask how you can help. Never let a self-serve customer leave feeling frustrated. Do all you can to make the experience a positive one. With phone and Internet customers, you may not know about a customer's problem until they have tried unsuccessfully and turn to you for help. Always leave them with a positive impression by giving your full attention, listening carefully, showing empathy, and taking care of their needs.

Make Sure Customers Are Satisfied

Asking a simple question such as "Did you find everything you needed?" or "Is there anything else I can do for you?" or "How is everything?" will help you know if your customers are satisfied. Of course, the best way to determine satisfaction is by observing your self-service customers during transactions and staying attentive. You will know by their facial expressions and body language whether they are comfortable or uncomfortable, at ease or frustrated. When you pay attention to your customers you should have a good idea of their satisfaction level. If, through body language, you think someone is not satisfied, ask "How can I help you?" Always offer your telephone and Internet self-serve customers a link to a live employee in the event they are not satisfied.

Thank Customers for Their Business

Always thank your customers for doing business with you. In person, say "Thank you for ____." Fill in the blank as appropriate: "coming in"; "doing business with us"; "being our customer." On the phone, include a thank you message before ending an automated contact. On websites, post a thank you or we appreciate your business message on the final screen.

PICTURE THIS...
THE RIGHT WAY TO END SELF-SERVICE CONTACTS

After Tina paid, she gathered her bags and was about to leave when Ted asked "Did everything else go okay for you?"

"Yes, thanks for all your help. I couldn't have done it without you," Tina said with a laugh.

"Those bunches of broccoli can really trip you up," Ted smiled warmly. "Thanks for coming in."

"Thank you for helping me." Tina walked out of the store completely satisfied with her experience. Her lasting impression of using the self-checkout was a positive one.

How Did the Customer Feel?

Tina felt valued when Ted asked if everything had gone okay. By easing her discomfort and making her feel comfortable, Tina felt that if this store cared enough to give such great service in a no-service situation, they truly cared about their customers. She had always liked shopping at the store for its convenience and the friendly employees; now she felt even more loyal about giving them her business.

PICTURE THIS...
PUTTING IT ALL TOGETHER

Tina stopped by the grocery store to pick up the items she needed to make dinner. This was part of her usual routine on her way home from work, and she usually did it with little thought: She'd run in, grab a basket, find the items on her list, and then find the shortest checkout line.

Today was different, though. For some reason, every checkout line had at least two people waiting with full carts. She looked over to the self-checkout area and noticed that one of the cash registers was available. She preferred letting a cashier check her out but decided to use self-serve after noticing a cashier standing at a podium in the self-check area.

Tina set her basket down on the shelf, and the cashier at the podium said "Hi, my name is Ted. I'll be right here if you need any help."

"Thank you," Tina replied.

Tina scanned the bar code on her first item and placed it in the bag. When she placed the second item in the bag, she heard a recorded voice saying "Place the item in the bag." *It is in the bag*, she thought. The voice sounded again. "Place the item in the bag."

"I don't know why that happens," Ted said as he walked over to Tina. "Sometimes the weight isn't picked up. Try picking up the can and putting it back in the bag."

Tina did as Ted suggested, and the voice stopped. Feeling a little embarrassed, she smiled at Ted. He noticed that someone was waiting to check out, so he backed up but stayed in the center of the checkout area.

Tina hurriedly picked up the next item in her basket, a bunch of broccoli. When she placed her broccoli on the scanner and looked confused, Ted walked back over to her. "The screen is going to prompt you to enter a four-digit number. If you can't find it on the produce, the items are listed on this roller." Ted pointed above the screen and showed Tina how to find broccoli.

"Thank you so much for helping me." Tina scanned the rest of her items.

After she paid, she gathered her bags and was about to leave when Ted asked "Did everything else go okay for you?"

"Yes, thanks for all your help. I couldn't have done it without you," Tina said with a laugh.

"Those bunches of broccoli can really trip you up," Ted smiled warmly. "Thanks for coming in."

"Thank you for helping me." Tina walked out of the store completely satisfied with her experience. Her lasting impression of using the self-checkout was a positive one.

Whether you provide service through traditional channels or by offering self-service options to your customers, you can always find ways to be courteous, communicate well, and build relationships. You can always find ways to give your customers more than they expect. Customers are not going to set high expectations when they serve themselves; when you give them the same consideration that you give your traditional customers, you show how much you value each and every one of your customers.

**BUSINESS
NØT
AS USUAL**

Always Give Customers More than They Expect, Even When They Do It Themselves

Many businesses are finding ways to integrate self-service options for their customers. Your business may be considering installing self-serve kiosks or checkout lanes. You may already have an automated phone answering system that provides options for customers to interact with the system without any human contact. You may provide a website for your customers to place orders, review account information, or pay bills.

There are many great reasons to implement self-service. Number one is that customers often prefer doing it themselves. Looking at it from a customer standpoint, you are providing a quick, efficient, and convenient way for them to do business with you. Looking at it from a business perspective, you can save time, money, and resources, and it allows you to redirect employees to other functions.

Whichever way you view your implementation of self-service, you can make the transition go smoothly by being available to train your customers how to use your self-service procedures and then ensuring that help is always available. Taking these steps will guarantee a long-lasting positive experience for both customers and employees.

Before implementing self-service options, plan how you will train and provide exceptional customer service to those customers who wish to serve themselves. Write down specific procedures and goals to help you through the transition phase. Remember: Making customers happy is your first priority.

- Always stay tuned in to your customers.

- Find innovative ways to stand out—positively—in your customers' minds.

- Include in your self-service goal plan ways to give your customers more than they expect.

KEY POINTS

Step 1: Welcome Your Customers

- Make it easy.

- Greet every customer.

- Be ready to help.

Step 2: Find the Best Solutions

- Monitor the flow.

- Look for teaching moments.
- Make your self-service customers feel valued.

Step 3: Show Appreciation

- Pay attention.
- Make sure customers are satisfied.
- Thank customers for their business.

PRACTICE LESSON

Refer to the customer contact example you wrote down at the beginning of the chapter.

Step 1: Welcome Your Customers

How will you greet self-service customers?

_____

_____

What can you say and do to let customers know you are available to help?

_____

_____

Step 2: Find the Best Solutions

What specific steps will you take to monitor the self-service flow?

_____

_____

How will you approach customers and what will you say to them when you see a teaching opportunity?

_____

_____

What can you do to make your self-service customers know you value them?

_____

_____

Step 3: Show Appreciation

What can you do to make sure your self-service customers are satisfied?

_____

_____

What will you say to customers when they are finished?

_____

_____

D O I N G   I T   R I G H T !

I appreciate the convenience of self-service options. When all goes right, I can get the job done quickly and efficiently. I can get in and out of my grocery store fast when I need only a few items. I can pay for and pump gas without waiting in line for a cashier to process my payment. ATMs are one of my favorite self-service options; I often wonder how I got by before I was able to get cash whenever I need it. I order airline tickets, book hotel reservations, and reserve rental cars. I can even order pizza my way online!

All in all, I think most consumers would agree that self-service has made life easier for us, which is a good thing in our speed-of-light-paced world.

So many self-serve options are available, it would be difficult for me to choose one that stands out. Perhaps a good example, for me, is the ability to interact with airline carriers online without having to involve a person. I prefer doing it myself because I know what dates and times work best for me. I often fly a particular airline and have found its site to be comprehensive and user-friendly. I make my flight reservations and actually enjoy interacting with the website and viewing my choices. If I do have a problem, I can dial the 800 number that is on the website and speak to an employee, usually with only a short delay in moving through the automated system. Every agent who has answered my phone calls has been friendly, courteous, and helpful.

I like that the airline emails me twenty-four hours before my flight, that it's time to check in. For some airports, I don't even have to print a ticket. I can use my cellphone at the check-in counter. When the mobile option isn't available, there is a notification on the website so I know that I need to print my tickets. Most airports offer kiosk check-in, and easily identified uniformed employees are available to offer assistance. If I choose to stand in line for an agent to help me, I never feel that I am bothering them.

While your company most likely is not as large as a major airline, the single most important thing you can do, if you provide self-service, is to make sure that the process is easy, that you offer help options, that you respond quickly to resolve problems, and that you provide exceptional customer service. Remember, self-service never means no-service. Self-service means finding ways to serve your customers when they aren't expecting service. When you successfully do that, they will be more likely to put your company on their favorites list.

H O W   D O   I   M E A S U R E   U P ?

1. When I handle self-service, do I greet every customer and let them know that I am available to help? What can I do to make sure I remember this step?

    _____

    _____

    _____

    _____

2. How effective and efficient am I in monitoring the flow of self-service customers? When I notice a teaching opportunity, what do I say to offer help? What can I do better?

    _____

    _____

    _____

    _____

3. How do I make sure all my customers are satisfied with their self-service experience? What do I need to do to improve in this area?

    _____

    _____

    _____

    _____

Calming the Storm:
Customer Complaint Contacts

EVERY CUSTOMER COMPLAINT IS AN
OPPORTUNITY TO MAKE THINGS BETTER

Write down a customer contact you handled in which a customer was dissatisfied with your company:

_____

_____

_____

_____

_____

Think about the scenario as you work through this chapter. Use it as the example when answering the Practice Lesson questions at the end of the chapter.

You have learned many valuable skills so far. You learned how to effectively communicate by listening and speaking well, and how to build relationships with customers. You learned the steps to interact successfully with customers in person, on the phone, through Internet and social media transactions, and in self-serve situations. You know how to welcome customers, handle their requests by finding the best solutions, and end interactions by showing appreciation. Congratulations! You have the necessary skills to handle customers successfully.

But what about those customers who are upset, angry, or agitated, and take their frustrations out on you? Complaining customers may rattle even the most competent, confident frontline employee. Learning how to deal with a complaining customer will give you the self-assurance to effectively help each and every one of your customers in any situation.

CUSTOMER SERVICE IS CUSTOMER COMPLAINT CONTACTS

Mistakes happen. Customers will complain. What is most important is what you do when customers are dissatisfied. In this chapter, you are going to learn the necessary skills to successfully handle these customers by understanding the reason for the complaint and knowing what you must do to rectify the situation. How well you are able to resolve complaints will make the difference in customers' perceptions of service. They will either feel gratified that you found a satisfactory outcome, or their negative feelings will increase. When that happens, they will continue complaining.

Customers may complain for a number of reasons. They may be upset about a delay in processing their requests, impatient about your company's response time, frustrated about having to call repeatedly about a problem, angry over something that was mishandled by an employee, or perhaps complaining is part of their personality. But typically, when a customer complains it is because his or her needs have not been met.

Handling customer complaint contacts requires special skills. Assuring the customer that you can help and then listening carefully will enable you to determine the reason for the complaint. When you investigate what went wrong, you will identify the cause of the problem, which will lead you to find the best solution. Thanking the customer for allowing you to make things right enables you to restore your relationship, and following up to make sure the customer is satisfied makes you stand out as someone who truly cares about customer service. Taking the extra step to analyze what went wrong helps to fix any practices or procedures that need to be fixed.

PICTURE THIS...
THE WRONG WAY TO HANDLE DIFFICULT CUSTOMERS

Mike is a service representative for an appliance repair company. He has held this job for five years and is experienced in handling customers. However, Mike does not feel comfortable handling customers who complain. He can easily become defensive. When he received a call from Mr. Roberts, the following happened:

"ABC Appliance Repair, this is Mike speaking."

"Mike, this is Mr. Roberts. My service contract number is ACH2234. I'm not very happy right now. I called first thing this morning, and you were supposed to send a service person before noon. Now it's twelve thirty, and no one's showed."

"Hold on," Mike responded with a slight tinge of rudeness in his voice.

"Hold on? I don't want to hold on. My time is valuable, and I don't have all day to wait around. I want to know how soon someone will be out."

"Mr. Roberts, you need to hold while I check on this for you. We don't make a habit of making appointments we can't keep. We don't normally tell people we'll be out if we don't have someone to send out."

"I'm telling you, someone was supposed to be here."

"I'm checking our records. . . . Okay, I see what happened. Looks like when you called this morning, we did tell you we could send a person out, but you said you were going to call back to schedule the service call. We have no record that you called us back. I can schedule you for service tomorrow."

"I'm not waiting until tomorrow. I told the employee I would call back if I couldn't rearrange my schedule. She told me I was scheduled for this morning. The appointment was set. Tomorrow isn't satisfactory. I want someone out now."

"Evidently you told the rep you were going to call back. That's what she noted on the record. If you had scheduled an appointment when you spoke to her, we would have sent someone out."

"I know what was said in our conversation, and I know I was scheduled for service this morning."

"Well, the soonest we can be out is tomorrow."

"Tomorrow isn't satisfactory. I've been sitting home all morning waiting for the service person."

"We don't have service people just sitting here waiting for calls. Everyone has already been dispatched today."

"Obviously I'm not getting through to you. I had an appointment for this morning. The person hasn't arrived. I need a person out this afternoon. Let me speak to a supervisor."

What Went Wrong?

In this contact, just about everything went wrong. When Mike received this call, all that was clear was that there had been a miscommunication. This was a case of he said/he or she said. Mike became defensive, sided with the employee, and spoke to the customer in a rude tone. When he blamed the customer for the miscommunication, Mr. Roberts asked for a supervisor.

How Did the Customer Feel?

Mr. Roberts became more upset as the conversation progressed. The manner in which Mike spoke to him, and then blamed him for causing the miscommunication, caused Mr. Roberts to feel that he needed a supervisor to handle his problem.

It is not always easy to know what to say or how to handle customers who are upset from the moment you begin your conversation. When a customer complains, there usually is a legitimate reason. By listening carefully and putting yourself in your customer's shoes, you will most likely be able to understand the reason he or she is upset. Master and practice the following five-step process, and you will have the tools you need to handle any customer in any situation:

Step 1: Understand the Complaint

Step 2: Identify the Cause

Step 3: Solve the Problem

Step 4: Restore the Relationship

Step 5: Fix What Needs to Be Fixed

In the contact with Mr. Roberts, Mike could have done many things differently. He should have been focused on solving the problem, rather than insinuating that the customer was at fault. His rude tone and defensive attitude were not what Mr. Roberts wanted to hear. Determining who was right and who was wrong was not important. What was important was Mr. Roberts' *perception* of the situation. Who is to blame should never matter when dealing with a customer who is voicing a complaint. Making the transition from an angry or upset customer to a satisfied customer should always be your number-one goal.

TIP

Communicate Effectively in Sticky Situations

You learned valuable communication skills that start by offering a warm welcome. But what happens when the customer's opening statement is to voice a complaint? Depending on the manner in which the customer speaks, you may be able to move through the steps easily; you may immediately become flustered; or, like Mike, you may become defensive. Customers complain in various ways. Some may speak calmly and voice their complaints in a logical manner. The other end of the spectrum is that some may yell, swear, become rude or belligerent, or speak incoherently.

Always stay calm. By remaining calm, you will be able to stay in control of the conversation. When you remain calm and speak in a controlled, neutral voice, the customer will begin to calm down. When you display confidence, the customer will begin to feel that you are going to take care of the problem.

Communicate appropriate verbal and nonverbal signals. Communication skills are important, especially in the beginning of the interaction, because you want to show the customer that you are going to find a satisfactory resolution. When face to face, make eye contact and keep your facial expressions concerned. Appearing confident, maintaining eye contact, keeping a relaxed stance, and using an assertive tone of voice all demonstrate that you are in control of the situation and are going to do your best to resolve the problem. When speaking by phone or writing, show concern in your tone of voice and the words you write. Keep your communication positive and helpful and always refrain from mimicking an angry or frustrated customer's demeanor.

STEP 1
UNDERSTAND THE COMPLAINT

Before you can begin resolving the problem, you must understand what it is. Listening carefully to the customer's opening statement will give you a good start. Restating what you thought you heard will give the customer the opportunity to clear up misunderstandings. Displaying empathy lets the customer know you are on his or her side.

Listen

Listen to the details of the problem without interrupting. Give the customer your undivided attention. Be patient and allow the customer to get it all out. It is up to you to discover the actual reason the customer is complaining, and that may be intermingled with the customer's emotions.

They may ramble, raise their voice, and be unable to clearly communicate their problem. Or they may want to voice their opinions on expected solutions as they explain the problem. Note the pertinent points, and ask clarifying questions if you are unsure. "Did I hear you correctly that we were supposed to be out by noon?" By actively listening to what the customer is saying rather than the way it is being said, you will be able to stay focused on understanding the problem.

Apologize

A customer who complains may often preface the complaint by voicing their emotions. "I'm really upset . . ." or "I'm angry about . . ." or "I'm so frustrated . . ." or "I'm ready to take my business elsewhere." Any time a customer conveys that he or she is not happy you should offer an apology, even if you feel you do not personally owe the customer an apology. You might say: "I'm sorry that happened" or "I feel terrible that happened to you." It is the right thing to do, whether or not your company is at fault. Whenever someone or something causes customers to be upset, apologizing will let them know you care.

Assure

Follow up your apology with an assurance that you are going to help. In your opening statement, tell the customer you will do what you can to resolve the problem. Doing so says that the buck stops with you. When you give your assurance up front, it can help put your customer in a different frame of mind.

Recap

The customer may articulate clearly; yet even if you feel you understand, you should recap. By recapping before going any further, you will make sure you have the correct interpretation, and it will help clear up any misunderstandings before you proceed. If the customer begins rambling, wait for a pause and then recap the problem to keep the focus on the situation rather than the emotions.

Display Empathy

Before you proceed, let the customer know that you understand his or her feelings. Reassure him or her again that you will help. Try to put yourself in your customer's shoes. No matter how a customer speaks to you, look at the problem from his or her perspective. You will be surprised how much clearer the problem will be when you see the situation from the customer's vantage point rather than your own.

TIP

In most cases, a complaining customer is not angry at you personally. Even if the customer refers to the company as "you," as Mr. Roberts did with Mike, and you know you personally were not the cause of the problem, remember that the customer sees you as the company. Focus solely on solving the problem to keep from becoming defensive.

PICTURE THIS...
THE RIGHT WAY TO UNDERSTAND THE COMPLAINT

"ABC Appliance Repair, this is Mike speaking."

"Mike, this is Mr. Roberts. My service contract number is ACH2234. I'm not very happy right now. I called first thing this morning, and you were supposed to send a service person before noon. Now it's twelve thirty and no one's showed."

"Mr. Roberts, I am so sorry about that. I'm going find out what happened and resolve this for you. You had a service appointment scheduled for this morning. Is that correct?"

"Yes, that's correct. I called first thing. The employee I spoke with told me she could send someone out this morning. I've been waiting all morning and no one came. I'm a busy person. I need someone out right away."

"I understand completely. Your time is valuable. I'll need to check our records to see what happened. Can you hold while I do that?"

"Yes, I'll hold."

How Did the Customer Feel?

Mr. Roberts appreciated that Mike listened carefully and displayed empathy when he said he understood his frustration. By apologizing and speaking confidently and assertively in a concerned tone, Mike enabled Mr. Roberts to start calming down. Mike recapped the complaint, which Mr. Roberts confirmed as correct. Mr. Roberts appreciated Mike's confident and calm demeanor, and he felt that Mike would work to resolve the problem.

TIP

If an angry customer immediately asks for your manager or the owner of your company without first giving you a chance to help, try this approach: "Ms. Customer, please give me the opportunity to resolve the problem. I'll do my best to take care of this for you, and if you are still not satisfied, I will personally refer your problem to my manager (or owner)." Your confident manner will give the customer the peace of mind that you are truly interested in resolving her problem.

If a customer uses profanity, calmly say "Mr. Customer, I understand you are upset, and I am going to help you, but there is no reason to use profanity." In most cases, the customer will stop. If it continues, calmly say "I am going to work with you to resolve your problem. Will you please explain to me what happened without using profanity?" Again, by maintaining a calm demeanor, your customer will begin to calm down.

STEP 2
IDENTIFY THE CAUSE

After you are certain you understand the reason for the complaint, your next step is to figure out the cause of the problem. In Mr. Roberts's case, Mike has a clear idea of the complaint. Mr. Roberts called earlier and scheduled a morning appointment. He was upset because it was past noon and no one had been out. Mike must now figure out what caused the problem.

Investigate the Situation

If the cause is not easily determined, you may pick up valuable clues by reading computer notes, checking with another department, or asking the employee who handled the customer previously. Mike asked Mr. Roberts to hold so he could find out what had happened. This allowed Mike some time to review Mr. Roberts's account record and the dispatch log. If, after asking a customer to hold, you find the investigation will take longer than a reasonable hold time, make a specific commitment to get back to the customer.

TIP

> When making a commitment to get back to the customer when you need to review some information, it is important to give a specific time frame rather than promising to call back "as soon as possible" or "right away." Terms like these mean different things to different people. "Right away" might mean sometime today to you; it could mean within fifteen minutes to your customer.
>
> Also, when promising to get back to a customer, think about the length of time you will need and offer a realistic time frame. If your customer is dissatisfied with the commitment, try saying "That's the best I can do in order to find out what happened."

Determine If the Customer Has a Valid Complaint

After investigating, you should be able to figure out whether the customer's complaint is legitimate. Most likely it will be. If you cannot determine a valid cause for the customer's complaint, it may be prudent to rule in favor of the customer, especially if this is a one-time complaint. If the customer is a chronic complainer for which there is no valid basis, ask your manager to make the call. In Mr. Roberts's situation, Mike did not know who was responsible for the miscommunication. He only knew that a misunderstanding had occurred between Mr. Roberts and the first employee. Mr. Roberts had expected a service person to be dispatched that morning. Mike should assume that Mr. Roberts's perception was correct.

Apologize Again If Necessary

If your investigation leads to the conclusion that someone or something within your company is at fault, take responsibility and apologize again. In any case, apologizing a second time reiterates your concern and desire to make things right with the customer.

Explain What Happened

Keep the emotion out of your voice and stick to the facts. Be truthful, even when it means saying your company has made a mistake. The customer may not like to hear what you are saying, but your honesty will be appreciated. Customers respect employees who are honest and up-front. Covering up, being evasive, or lying is never a good business policy.

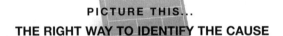

PICTURE THIS...
THE RIGHT WAY TO IDENTIFY THE CAUSE

"Mr. Roberts, thank you for holding. I checked our records and, again, I apologize that we weren't out this morning. When you spoke to the employee earlier, she was under the assumption that you needed to call back to schedule your appointment. We didn't hear back from you and therefore never scheduled the service call."

How Did the Customer Feel?

Mike took the time to investigate and determined from the computer notes that the customer had said he would call back to schedule. Since Mike had not spoken to Mr. Roberts on the first call, he had no way of knowing what was actually said. He could not determine whether the customer's complaint was valid since it was the result of a miscommunication.
He apologized and stayed neutral when he explained what had happened. By staying neutral, Mike did not take or assign blame, and that helped Mr. Roberts calm down.

Making the decision to say "no" to a customer's demands should never be made lightly, yet pacifying customers who do not have valid complaints can become costly. Only your manager and the company's owner know what price the company can afford to pay to retain a customer.

Each case will be different; your manager may need to decide which customers are worth the effort. What are some situations that arise in your business where a customer has no basis for his or her complaint? Think about the following questions and come up with some guidelines for handling these particular situations:

- Is this a one-time complaint, or is the customer a chronic complainer?

- Does the customer complain in order to receive special favors?

- Does the customer do enough business with your company to make the aggravation worthwhile?

- Is this person a new customer you want to keep?

There will be occasions when there is a possibility that saying "no" will cause the customer to end the business relationship. There will be occasions when it is not cost-effective to keep doing business with a customer who requires more than you can afford to satisfy. In these cases, your manager should make the final decision and handle ending the business relationship.

STEP 3
SOLVE THE PROBLEM

You have investigated and determined the cause of the problem. Now it is time to offer a solution. If you can rectify the problem to the customer's satisfaction, you get off easy: "Mr. Roberts, we have a service person who just called in. We're dispatching her to your home, and she'll be there within fifteen minutes."

More than likely, that is not going to be the case and you are going to offer a solution your customer does not want to hear. What you say and how you say it will make a big difference in the customer's response.

Offer Your Best Solution

This is not the time to offer something mediocre and begin a bartering session for a better solution. By offering the best you can do, you will sound confident when presenting your solution. Speak clearly and explain specifically what you are able to do to resolve the problem. If you are handling a customer who is extremely upset or angry, take a deep breath to calm your nerves, and think about what you will say before proceeding. Taking the time to adequately explain your solution will help you communicate more effectively. Tell the customer *what* you can do and also explain *why* that is your best solution.

Focus on What You Can Do

Always focus on the positive and state what you are able to do, rather than on what you cannot do. In the case of Mr. Roberts, all the service people had already been dispatched for the day, so sending someone out in the afternoon was not an option. What could Mike do for him? Before offering the solution, perhaps Mike could check with his dispatcher to see if he could schedule a service call for the first appointment the next morning. While this was not a solution that Mr. Roberts was going to embrace, it would narrow his wait time and show him that Mike was doing all he could to expedite the request.

Never Assign Blame

When you offer your solution, do not fault the customer. When you are trying to help a customer who is not happy, blaming is never wise. Likewise, never shirk responsibility by blaming another employee or department. Saying "The first employee you spoke with messed up and should have scheduled your appointment" may relieve you from personal responsibility, but it does nothing to make the customer feel better.

Always remember that to the customer, you are the company. Use "I" or "we" when referring to your company to show that you are accountable.

Show Compassion

If the customer expresses dissatisfaction, let him or her know that you understand. Compassion and understanding can help mend a damaged relationship. You may not be able to fix the problem in the precise manner in which the customer would like, but at least you can show that you care.

Offer an Alternative Solution

Your best solution will not always appease the customer. Customers sometimes have unrealistic expectations. They are likely to expect the problem to be resolved immediately, and that is often impossible. If your best solution is not suitable to the customer, try to find something that will work. If you are at a loss to know how to resolve a problem, ask for the customer's input as to what will work, and then work together to come up with a realistic solution that is mutually acceptable.

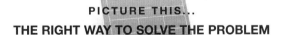

PICTURE THIS...
THE RIGHT WAY TO SOLVE THE PROBLEM

"All our service people have already been dispatched for today, but here's what I can do for you. I checked with our dispatch department to get you the soonest appointment possible. We can schedule you for the first appointment tomorrow. Someone will be out before nine."

"I want someone out today."

"I understand how you feel. If I had waited all morning, I'd be upset too. I wish I could change what took place on your first phone call. I told my dispatcher what happened and asked if there was any way we could free someone up today. Unfortunately, we're completely booked, and he said there is no chance we can do that. The best I can do is the first appointment tomorrow. I know this isn't what you were hoping for, but I'm doing my best for you."

"You said the person will be here before nine?"

"Yes. We already have you set up. I get in at eight tomorrow, and I'll personally follow up on this to make sure nothing goes wrong again."

"Well, I guess tomorrow first thing is the best you can do."

"Yes, sir, it is."

How Did the Customer Feel?

Mr. Roberts appreciated Mike's honest and sincere answer. When Mike spoke in a confident manner and focused on what he could do, Mr. Roberts understood that Mike was doing his best. Mr. Roberts also appreciated Mike's understanding as to why he was upset.

BRAINSTORM

What happens when a customer has a legitimate complaint that you cannot resolve to his or her satisfaction? What if Mr. Roberts still demanded an appointment today?

Discuss situations in which you were unable to find a satisfactory solution to a customer's problem, as well as how you should handle cases in which the customers' requests are impossible to satisfy. Talk about the following questions and come up with some "best-solution" guidelines.

- What alternative solutions can you offer customers?

- What should you say to customers when you cannot find a satisfactory solution?

- At what point should you involve your manager (or owner)?

There may be times when, no matter what you offer, your solution will not be acceptable. When this happens, make sure to say that you appreciate and understand the customer's point of view, that you did your best, and that you are sorry you were not able to work out a satisfactory solution.

STEP 4
RESTORE THE RELATIONSHIP

What you say next can go a long way in mending a broken relationship. When a customer's trust in your company is damaged, you lose credibility. It is important to tell your customers that you value their business and want to restore your relationship with them. This step should not take that long, yet it may be the most important step in handling customer complaints. Showing appreciation and following up will make a positive difference with your customers.

Thank the Customer for Allowing You to Make Things Right

You cannot take back what has happened, but you can say something to let your customers know you value them as much as you value their business. After you satisfactorily resolve a customer's problem, go one step further and thank them for their understanding.

Offer Something Extra

If you feel it is warranted, offer some sort of compensation or restitution. This is not something you need to do every time a customer complains. Rather, offer something extra when you feel the mistake has greatly affected the customer. Doing this will not make the problem go away, but it reinforces the fact that you appreciate the customer. Some examples may be: priority handling, credit toward a service charge or fees rendered, or a discount on a future purchase.

Make a Follow-Up Call or Visit

As a courtesy to your customer, follow up to make sure the solution was satisfactory. Think about this: Customers often take their business elsewhere without telling you they are dissatisfied. Every time this happens, you lose a valued customer. When customers take the time to tell you about a problem, give them the time by making sure your resolution was satisfactory.

PICTURE THIS...
THE RIGHT WAY TO RESTORE THE RELATIONSHIP

"Mr. Roberts, thank you for giving us an opportunity to resolve your problem."

The next afternoon, Mike spoke with Mr. Roberts again:

"Mr. Roberts, this is Mike from ABC. I wanted to check back with you and make sure the service person was out this morning and fixed the problem."

"Yes, Mike, she was out first thing and everything is fine now. Thanks for calling me back."

How Did the Customer Feel?

Mr. Roberts felt valued when Mike thanked him for allowing him to fix the problem. He was pleasantly surprised by the follow-up call, and his confidence in ABC was restored.

STEP 5
FIX WHAT NEEDS TO BE FIXED

You know that mistakes are going to happen. No one, not even a business, can be expected to do things correctly one hundred percent of the time. When you take care of a customer's problem to their satisfaction, you feel good; but unless you analyze what happened and fix what went wrong, the same type of problem is likely to happen again. Repeatedly taking care of the same type of problems will only lead to frustration, both for you and for your customers.

Analyze What Went Wrong

When you resolve a customer's complaint, think about what caused it. Was it a random occurrence? Or have you handled the same problem before? In the event that you are correcting repeated problems, get to the root of the issue. Is it caused by employee error? Does another department have a different understanding than yours? Do your company policies make it difficult for customers?

Fix the Problem

When you determine what is repeatedly causing a problem, you are in the best position to fix it. Suppose Mike had handled similar issues by the same employee. He could speak to the employee about what was occurring. Perhaps he determined that there was a system error in the program that scheduled the appointments. He could speak to his manager to get the error corrected. As your company's chief communicator, you are in the best position to know what needs to be fixed. Any time you notice aspects of your business operations that customers have valid complaints about, talk to your manager.

Make Things Better

Your primary goal should always be to make it easy for your customers to do business with your company. When it is easy for customers to do business with you, it is easier for you to satisfy them. When you are part of the solution, you will be more satisfied with the work you do. As the voice for your company and customers, you can make a difference.

BRAINSTORM

If you cannot easily determine which areas make it difficult for your customers to do business with you, try this. Do a "walk-through" of each step of a customer interaction. Look at your company from a customer's perspective. Discuss any areas that make it difficult for your customers to do business with you. Try to come up with ways to change those areas, and rewrite your company's policies to address them. Think about the following questions and come up with some guidelines:

- How easy is it for customers to do business with you?

- Which of your policies make it difficult to satisfy your customers?

- In what areas of your business do you get repeat complaints?

PICTURE THIS...
PUTTING IT ALL TOGETHER

"ABC Appliance Repair, this is Mike speaking."

"Mike, this is Mr. Roberts. My service contract number is ACH2234. I'm not very happy right now. I called first thing this morning, and you were supposed to send a service person before noon. Now it's twelve thirty and no one's showed."

"Mr. Roberts, I am so sorry about that. I'm going find out what happened and resolve this for you. You had a service appointment scheduled for this morning. Is that correct?"

"Yes, that's correct. I called first thing. The employee I spoke with told me she could send someone out this morning. I've been waiting all morning and no one came. I'm a busy person. I need someone out right away."

"I understand completely. Your time is valuable. I'll need to check our records to see what happened. Can you hold while I do that?"

"Yes, I'll hold."

After a short delay, Mike returned to the call and said: "Mr. Roberts, thank you for holding. I checked our records and, again, I apologize that we weren't out this morning. When you spoke to the employee earlier, she was under the assumption that you needed to call back to schedule your appointment. We didn't hear back from you and therefore never scheduled the service call.

"All our service people have already been dispatched for today, but here's what I can do for you. I checked with our dispatch department to get you the earliest possible appointment. We can schedule you for the first appointment tomorrow. Someone will be out before nine."

"I want someone out here today."

"I understand how you feel. If I'd waited all morning, I'd be upset too. I wish I could change what happened on your first phone call. I told my dispatcher what has happened and asked if there was any way we could free someone up today. Unfortunately, we're completely booked, and he said there is no chance we can do that. The best I can do is the first appointment tomorrow. I know this isn't what you were hoping for, but I'm doing my best for you."

"You said the person will be here before nine?"

"Yes, we already have you set up. I get in at eight tomorrow, and I'll personally follow up on this to make sure nothing goes wrong again."

"Well, I guess tomorrow first thing is the best you can do."

"Yes, sir, it is."

The next afternoon, Mike called Mr. Roberts: "Mr. Roberts, this is Mike from ABC. I wanted to check back with you to make sure the service person who was out this morning fixed the problem."

"Yes, Mike, she was out first thing and everything is fine now. Thanks for calling me back."

When you master the steps for handling complaints, you will gain the confidence to positively handle any scenario. When you have confidence in your ability, it will be reflected in the way in which you deal with your customers. When you are confident in yourself, your customers will be confident in your ability to do your best for them.

The bottom line is that when you deal with customers, there are going to be problems. Whether the problem is caused by the customer or by the company, what is important in any customer complaint contact is what you do to resolve the problem and how valued you make the customer feel.

Every Customer Complaint Is an Opportunity to Make Things Better

Looking for opportunities to improve is always important. Think about this: If you don't satisfy your customers, they are going to find a business that does.

Do you know that the most common reason customers take their business elsewhere is due to mistreatment by frontline employees? And the sad news is that most of the time, customers won't even complain. They just won't come back.

When customers take the time to complain, they are giving you a gift. They are giving you the opportunity to make the situation right. When you do so, you will not only save this customer, you also save others who would not have taken the time to tell you when something is wrong.

When you take the time to satisfy even the most difficult customers, you increase your chances of making it through difficult times.

- Make sure your attitude is never indifferent, but one of making a difference.

- Put yourself in your customers' shoes and try to see things from their perspective.

- Focus on the problem, not the person's attitude or behavior.

- Display empathy toward the customer's situation.

- Focus on what you *can* do.

K E Y   P O I N T S

Step 1: Understand the Complaint

- Listen.

- Apologize.

- Assure.

- Recap.

- Display empathy.

Step 2: Identify the Cause

- Investigate the situation.

- Determine if the customer has a valid complaint.

- Apologize again if necessary.

- Explain what happened.

Step 3: Solve the Problem

- Offer your best solution.

- Focus on what you can do.
- Never assign blame.
- Show compassion.
- Offer an alternative solution.

Step 4: Restore the Relationship

- Thank the customer for allowing you to make things right.
- Offer something extra.
- Make a follow-up call or visit.

Step 5: Fix What Needs to Be Fixed

- Analyze what went wrong.
- Fix the problem.
- Make things better.

P R A C T I C E   L E S S O N

Refer to the customer contact example you wrote down at the beginning of the chapter.

Step 1: Understand the Complaint

Write down the customer's opening statement.

_____

_____

Write a statement of regret and assurance. Recap the customer's opening statement to ensure your understanding.

_____

_____

How will you display empathy?

_____

_____

Step 2: Identify the Cause

Assume that you are going to need to research further and will need to call the customer back. Write an example of how you will state the commitment.

_____

_____

Write a statement explaining what happened.

_____

_____

Step 3: Solve the Problem

Write a statement telling the customer what you can do to solve the problem.

_____

_____

If the customer objects, write a statement offering empathy.

_____

_____

Assume this customer is not satisfied with your resolution. Write an alternate solution you could offer.

_____

_____

Step 4: Restore the Relationship

Write a statement thanking the customer for allowing you to correct the problem.

_____

_____

Was this problem caused by your company? Remember to leave your customer with a good impression of yourself and your business by offering some sort of compensation or restitution. What will you offer this customer?

_____

_____

What will you say to the customer in your follow-up call?

_____

_____

Step 5: Fix What Needs to Be Fixed

Think about this situation. Analyze what went wrong. What can be changed to avoid similar problems in the future? Write out what changes you will make.

_____

_____

Remember, the important thing to keep in mind is to always strive to make it easy for your customers to do business with you.

D O I N G   I T   R I G H T !

In Chapter 6, I used an example of an irate customer posting a Twitter complaint. Actually, that customer was me. I had an upcoming business trip and needed an outfit for a dinner gala. I had no time to shop locally, so I went online and found something I liked at a large clothing retailer. I ordered the outfit and upgraded shipping to the two-day option. After the order was shipped, I checked tracking and noticed that the delivery date was for the following Tuesday, which happened to be three days beyond the specified two-day interval. And to make matters worse, Tuesday was my travel date.

I called the retailer and the employee with whom I spoke assured me that my order would be delivered the following day, Friday. I asked him if he was certain of that, since tracking is usually accurate. He assured me it was so.

The next morning, I again checked tracking. It still showed the following Tuesday. I called again, and the employee placed me on hold so she could check. When she came back online, she said she had contacted UPS, they were rerouting my package, and that it would indeed be delivered that day. I was incredulous when she told me this, because I knew without a doubt that she was not being truthful. I challenged her whether she had called UPS in Phoenix, where the tracking showed the item was located. She said yes. I questioned her again. Yes, came the emphatic answer. Then she assured me, *don't worry, it will be there today.*

I knew it wouldn't. I felt very angry knowing that not one, but two employees had given me false information. I called back and asked for a supervisor, who confirmed that the delivery was in fact Tuesday. She apologized but offered no additional help.

I always strive to write good-news customer service stories and would have preferred posting a commendation, but this incident made me so upset that I posted a complaint on Twitter. Here is what I posted: *@[name of retailer] Terrible customer service. Placed an expedited order, was sent normal. 2 reps said delivery tom. Supv confirmed no.*

I remember thinking *Well, that's that*. I got it off my chest. It made me feel slightly better being able to vent, even if I was venting to no one in particular and thinking that nothing would come of it. So I was extremely surprised (and heartened) when, within thirty minutes of my post, I received the following message from the retailer:

> *@ReneeEvenson We're disappointed to hear this, Renee—would you DM us your email address & more details? We will do our best to help!*

I wrote out the details of my complaint and sent a direct message. After a back-and-forth exchange, the employee apologized for the misinformation and offered to ship the order to my travel destination, which I declined. She rerouted the existing order back to their facility and immediately credited me for that. I still had one issue that needed to be addressed. Not one, but two employees, took the easy route by paying lip service rather than being factual. The employee replied:

> *I do sincerely apologize for the customer service that you received from our company. I will definitely forward your concerns to the managers here, and we will use this information to coach our agents to prevent further situations such as this. Because of the mistakes that occurred on our end, we are giving you 25% off a future order. I'm very sorry for this issue.*

So even though I didn't receive the outfit, I appreciated that the retailer did what it could to rectify the situation by offering to ship to my travel destination. Because the error was preventable, the employee offered me compensation toward a future purchase. All is good between the retailer and me. But the moral of the story is that if it had not responded, all would not be good. There are a lot of retailers from which I could choose.

In business, it is a fact of life that problems will occur. It's how you handle problems that makes all the difference to your customers. Whether you are a small business or a large retailer, handling any situation to your customer's satisfaction and taking the extra step to restore the relationship will keep that relationship strong.

H O W   D O   I   M E A S U R E   U P ?

1. How good am I at remaining calm and in control when customers yell, or speak rudely or angrily? What can I do to improve?

---

2. When working to resolve a problem, how well do I focus on what I can do? If the customer is not satisfied with my recommendation, what can I do to find alternative solutions?

---

3. Do I always remember to thank the customer for giving me the opportunity to make things right? What else do I do that sets my company and me apart and helps to restore our relationship?

PART THREE

PUTTING IT ALL TOGETHER

9

Hitting the Ground Running: Ready, Set, Go

**BEING GOOD AT WHAT YOU DO
MAKES DOING IT A PLEASURE**

You have covered a lot of ground in this book. Part I focused on putting your best face forward. You learned how to present yourself by using basic courtesies, by communicating effectively, and by building strong relationships. Part II focused on putting your customers first. You learned special skills to handle customers in person, on the telephone, through online and social media, and in self-service settings. You learned how to successfully handle customer complaints.

Now it is time to put it all together. You are on your way to giving great customer service. Where do you go from here?

CUSTOMER SERVICE IS BEING READY AND SET TO GO

Depending on your comfort level, you may either be ready to jump into the customer service fray with both feet or you may only be ready to take your first steps. If you feel a little overwhelmed by all that you have learned, you are not alone. Not everyone will be ready for that huge step. Do not feel self-conscious about beginning by taking small steps. In fact, even if you feel confident that you are ready to apply everything you have learned, it might be a good idea for you to focus on one area at a time so that you can turn each of these lessons into a lifelong habit.

Review Your List of Learning Outcomes

If you feel unsure about any of the material, review the relevant chapters again. Go back over those sections of the training until you feel comfortable applying the material to your customer situations. If you still feel uncomfortable with any of the steps, discuss them with your manager. To get the most out of this training, it is important that you feel confident about the total package.

Start with the Basics

Focus on the way you present yourself when people are forming their first impressions of you. Get used to using courtesy words and phrases: please, thank you, excuse me, I'm sorry, yes, and so on. When you find yourself using these words without conscious effort, turn your attention to your attitude. Remember that your attitude includes how you talk to yourself, so always use positive words in your self-talk. Review the right way to handle sticky situations and form the habit of acting in an ethical manner at all times.

When You Are Comfortable with the Basics, Focus on Communicating Effectively

Think before you speak so you will say what you mean and mean what you say. Pay attention to the nonverbal messages you send by developing an awareness of your body language, facial expressions, gestures, and voice tone. Next, focus on your questioning skills. It may help to write down some sample open and closed questions that you frequently use. Review them often so you will become comfortable asking them. Remember that no matter what type of question a customer asks you, you should always try to give more than a one-word answer. Find ways to give your customers more than they ask for. When customers say no, find out the reason and offer the best solution based on each customer's needs. Finally, and most important, listen attentively. As your company's chief communicator, listening is the most important skill to master when you communicate with customers. Be aware of the barriers that make listening difficult, because unless you listen well, you are not going to know what is best for each customer.

Build Strong Relationships with Your Customers

Now that you have learned the nuts and bolts of communicating effectively, it is time to let your personality shine. Establish rapport by being friendly and interested in your customers in order to find common ground. Once you establish rapport, you will feel more comfortable interacting positively with them. Developing a comfort level with your customers will enable you to help each customer by identifying individual needs. When you do these things, you will make your customers feel valued. When customers feel valued, they are more likely to do repeat business with you and your company. The last thing you learned about relationships is that not all customers are the same. You learned how to deal with different personality types, people from different cultures, and people with disabilities. The most important thing to remember is to treat all your customers the way you like to be treated.

Practice Each of These Steps

Each one is a building block you add to your customer service foundation. By the time you feel comfortable using all the principles learned in Part I, you will have built a strong foundation. Practice using them not only at work, but also in your interactions with family and friends. Practice using them in situations in which you are the customer. Learning how to behave courteously and communicate well will help you build positive relationships in all areas of your life.

Put Your Customers First

Practicing the skills you learned in Part I will help you take a huge step in the right direction, whether you handle customers face-to-face, by telephone, online, through social media, or in self-service settings. Forming a customer-first mindset is going to help you confidently handle customer complaints. When you display courteous words and behaviors, communicate effectively, and work to build strong relationships, you firmly cement together your customer service skills to help any customer in any situation.

Warmly welcoming customers into your business helps form a positive first impression, whether you are face-to-face with your customers or they are serving themselves. Conveying your willingness to help and maintaining a positive attitude will help you assist your customers, whether you are emailing, responding to social media posts, or speaking by phone. Finding the best solution for each customer and ensuring that they are satisfied before ending your contacts will help you build solid relationships that result in loyal customers in every type of customer interaction.

Review These Steps Frequently

The more you use the principles you learned in Part I, the more comfortable and confident you will be when you apply them to the various types of customer interactions you learned in Part II. Reviewing the steps helps you cement your foundation with a strong bond on which to build your customer service skills. If your foundation is built on anything but concrete principles, it can easily crumble at any time. You may fall into old habits. You may form poor habits. By reviewing each section of this training from time to time, you guarantee you are maintaining a strong foundation of exceptional customer service habits.

YOUR CUSTOMER SERVICE TRAINING QUICK REFERENCE

Refer to the quick reference list that follows frequently to make sure you remember to follow all the lessons you learned.

The Basics

- First impressions matter.

- Courtesy counts.

- Attitude is everything.

- Do the right thing at all times.

Effective Communication

- Say what you mean and mean what you say.

- Enhance your messages with nonverbal techniques.

- Use correct grammar.

- Ask the correct questions and answer the questions correctly.

- Overcome the big no.

- Listen attentively.

Relationship Building

- Establish rapport.

- Interact positively with customers.

- Identify customers' needs.

- Make customers feel valued.

- Maintain ongoing relationships.

- Understand various types of customers.

Face-to-Face, Telephone, Online and Social Media, and Self-Service Contacts

- Welcome your customers.

- Handle customer requests by finding the best solutions.

- End interactions by showing appreciation.

Customer-Complaint Contacts

- Understand the complaint.

- Identify the cause.

- Solve the problem.

- Restore the relationship.

- Fix what needs to be fixed.

10

Being the Best You Can Be: The Total Package

ALWAYS LOOK FOR WAYS TO MAKE YOURSELF BETTER

Ready, set? Before you go, there is just one more step to take. You have read an entire book devoted to helping you give exceptional customer service. This last chapter is devoted to you, to help you be the best you can be in everything you do.

CUSTOMER SERVICE IS BEING THE BEST YOU CAN BE EVERY DAY

When you focus on being your best every day, good things happen. People will notice. They will respond more positively. They will respect you. You will perform better at work. You will seek out ways to give more of yourself to others. You will find happiness and satisfaction in all you do.

Take Responsibility for Your Actions

There is only one person in charge of you. That person is you. You control your actions. You control your performance at work. You control your behavior. You make the decisions for and about yourself. When you make the decision to be your best at all times, you will strive to achieve your best. You will feel good about the choices you make. You will feel good about yourself. When you feel good about yourself, you will reflect those feelings outward.

Become the Person You Want to Be

Create in your mind a positive vision of the person you want to become. If you have trouble seeing clearly, take time to focus on the qualities you want to personify. Envision the "you" you want to be. Picture yourself behaving this way and keep this vision in your consciousness. Change your self-talk to reflect the new you. If your vision is to be more confident, look in the mirror, smile at your reflection, and say out loud: "I am confident." Picture yourself acting in a confident manner. Then act this way. Initially it will be difficult and awkward; but the more you practice, the easier it will become until one day these behaviors will be second nature and you will no longer need to act the part.

Set Goals for Yourself

What will it take for you to become the person you envision yourself being? Do you need to go back to school? Do you need to join an organization that fosters the qualities you wish to exemplify? Write down specific goals. There is something magical about writing your goals on paper. Once they are written, you will be more focused on finding ways to achieve them. If some of your goals are too big or long-range, break them down into smaller, more manageable goals.

Keep Looking Forward

It is easy to get mired in the day-to-day grind. It is also easy to get mired in dwelling on the past. When you keep looking forward, it becomes easier to continue focusing on your goals. Self-talk is important. You cannot change what has already happened, but next time you can do things differently. Change your self-talk to words that will help you view yourself more positively. Respect yourself by being respectful of the way you talk to yourself.

Measure Your Own Level of Performance

Periodically, answer the following questions. Do I feel good, both physically and mentally? Am I happy, both in my job and in my life? Do I look forward to each day, going to work and doing other activities? Am I proud of my efforts? If most of your answers were "yes," you are likely performing well at work and working toward achieving your goals. If most of your answers were "no," it is time for self-reflection. Look inward to figure out the cause and determine what you can do to improve yourself and your situation. This might mean rethinking your goals. It may be time to create a more realistic vision of your future so you can set goals that are attainable.

Keep Striving

To be your best means to keep striving to be even better. Be curious. Ask questions. Try to learn something new every day. Learn from every experience. Develop resiliency. When something bad happens, analyze why it happened to learn how to keep it from happening again. Do not repeat the same mistake twice. Ask for advice when you need help. Try to anticipate problems before they get out of hand.

Be part of the solution, rather than part of the problem. Give your all in everything you do and take the extra step for your customers, your family, and your friends.

Be a Good Listener

This theme has been stressed throughout the book, and that's because it is the most important quality you can develop. Listening completely and attentively is important, not only in work situations but in every life situation. Being a good listener helps make you a good communicator. When you listen well, you know how to respond appropriately. You become well informed. You learn more. So put your phone down when you are with others, and tune in to them.

Have Fun Every Day

Being the best you can be has a positive reward: You begin enjoying everything you do. Maintain a positive attitude. Find the good in others. When someone is being difficult, whether it is a customer, friend, or significant other, do whatever you can to make that person's day better. When you encounter a stranger, smile. Be grateful that you have this day. Be appreciative of those around you. Laugh often. Stay positive. Enjoy today.

ALWAYS BE YOUR BEST!

The Essence of Customer Service Is Having HEART

The character of a person is found deep in the heart.

- **Honesty:** Tell the truth. Do the right thing. Be trustworthy.

- **Empathy:** Put yourself in the other person's shoes. Listen. Care.

- **Appreciation:** Look for the good in people. Express gratitude.

- **Respect:** Show care, concern, and consideration.

- **Tolerance:** Rather than judging others, accept their differences.

INDEX

H. 1/18